PRAISE FOR
hello, FEARS

"Michelle's radiant positive energy shines through these fresh pages of honest, quirky, and inspiring personal discovery. She delivers a powerful, practical playbook for slaying your self-doubt and unleashing the daring dreamer within."

—JOHN JACOBS, cofounder and chief creative optimist of The Life is Good Company

"Michelle's book shows us just how beautifully our lives can expand when we bust through our comfort zone, show up as our full selves, and dare to say Hello! to our fears. A critical guidebook for courageous living."

—PIERA GELARDI, executive creative director and cofounder of Refinery29

"No one has broken through more self-made limits than Michelle Poler, and that makes her uniquely equipped to help you smash through yours! This book is your secret weapon for demolishing your comfort zones and finally reaching your full potential."

—ANDY J. PIZZA, host of Creative Pep Talk podcast

"With a mix of humor and vulnerability, Michelle shows us what can happen when we focus on the best outcomes and become our authentic selves!"

—JESSICA WALSH, founder and creative director of &Walsh, cocreator and coauthor of 40 Days of Dating

Celebrity testimonials are great, but real people's testimonials are what I care about the MOST. Here are some of the most powerful messages we've received so far from those who read my content on a daily basis. This are real people: like you, like me.

"Michelle's message of embracing the serendipity of life's unpredictable nature by facing our uncomfortable fears with enthusiasm is essential for all of us who want to live a memorable and full life. If you are happy to stay stuck in the status quo, DO NOT READ THIS BOOK."
—KIRSTEN ANDERSON, playologist

"Michelle is the friend we all need—the one who pushes you to go for your dreams and give the best of yourself to the world unapologetically. Authentic, refreshing, and incredibly delightful, you can't help but fall in love with her and thank her (over and over again) for her no-nonsense wisdom in helping you face your fears and do it anyway! A must-read for anyone wanting to live fully."
—YAEL TRUSCH, Jewish Latin princess

"Discovering Michelle was actually was one of the most meaningful serendipities of my life. Her message shook me to the core... Now I can say: hello life and hello fears! You need to let this book impact your life as her message impacted mine."

—ANDREINA BRUNETTI, serendipity lover

"Michelle's message will inspire you to down the rules of your life, take hold of what others expect, and ask yourself what do YOU expect. What do you want out of this life? It can feel scary and it may not always be smooth, but Michelle shows it is *always* worth it."

—TERA WAGES, bow tie wearer

"Michelle shows us what a girl is capable of when she believes in herself. She has helped me find my own voice, face the fear of criticism, and set an example to my daughter. And that makes me feel like the happiest mom in the world."

—VIRGINIA HERRERA, happy mom

hello, FEARS

CRUSH your COMFORT ZONE and become who YOU'RE MEANT TO BE

MICHELLE POLER

sourcebooks

Published by Sourcebooks
P.O. Box 4410, Naperville, Illinois 60567-4410
(630) 961-3900
sourcebooks.com

Library of Congress Cataloging-in-Publication data is on file with the publisher.

Printed and bound in China.
PP 10 9 8 7 6 5 4 3

DEDICATED TO MY FUTURE KIDS *

⭐ Or maybe I should just dedicate this book to Adam, who actually exists now and was the reason why I was able to turn my life upside down like a delicious pancake.

⭐ ⭐ On that note, I'd like to dedicate this book to all the men out there who support and empower women.

CONTENTS

The one where I screw up
my Netflix talk & tackle
"personal fears"

WHATEVER YOU DO,
READ THIS CHAPTER

The one about Adam
quitting his job & stepping
forward into growth

The one about
making it real big

The one about
becoming the
most assertive
person you know

The one about using
our past to uncover
our purpose

INTRODUCTION: *Hello!*

I DON'T LIKE INTRODUCTIONS. I feel like I have to give away ALL the *good stuff* just to convince you that I'm worth reading. I'm a storyteller, so I don't want to JUST give away the fact that I faced one hundred... Come on! Don't make me say it. It will totally ruin the story.

Curious yet?

Fine, I'll spill. I did this project not too long ago as part of my master's degree in branding, with the hopes of becoming a braver person. I faced 100 fears in 100 days. And it worked! I became a braver person, and the challenge went viral. By facing my darkest fears, like jumping out of airplanes, dancing alone in bustling Times Square, eating gross oysters (still gross), I also inspired millions of people along the way. This was never part of my goal. I'm not *that* good of a person.

But convincing someone to read my book, buy my stuff? I'm still very afraid of doing that. I'm just a girl from Venezuela, living in New York, facing fears for a living, mostly the fear of public speaking, which I get paid to face over and over again.

But that's exactly why my voice could matter to you. That experience changed my life—and this book could change yours.

This book is not about a 100-day project. This book is about how I was able to go from being a fearful girl who was UNWILLING to get out of her comfort zone to being a fearful girl who was able to redefine the concepts of failing, rejection, fear as obstacle, criticism, and others' expectations and grow from there. Still a fearful woman, sure, but one who is checking her own boxes and living life according to her *own* standards now. Sometimes scared to try new things, but way more terrified of not even trying at all.

Would you dare to embrace that fear too?

This book is personal, both for me and for you. I tell stories here that I've never told before, I say pretty embarrassing and vulnerable things, and I kinda expect you to do the same—I mean #equality! The less we fool ourselves with what we believe others want to hear, the more we're able to uncover who we truly are. This book will help you embrace that message and evolve into becoming the best version of yourself. Isn't that one of the benefits of being alive?

You can turn this book to any chapter and begin from there. There are exercises I want you to work on as we go, and I want you to reflect and write in your own words and apply directly to your own life. This is not one of those books that you will read and pass on to someone else–nope! They can get their own books, darling; this one is yours to keep. You will want to revisit it at different stages of life and will get different things out of it each time you return. Fear will always be there, so continually changing our perceptions of it will help us go through life choosing courage and growth consistently. This book will get you outside of your comfort zone, and that's where all the magic happens, right?

OMG that's SO forking cliché! I hate introductions, so PLEASE let's get this over with. Are you ready? See you in Chapter 1, or 5, or 10, whichever you decide to read first!

XOXO,

Michelle

(MAKING IT UP
AS I GO SINCE 1988)

hello, LIFE

FROM AUTOPILOT TO LIVING FULLY

I'M BACKSTAGE, STANDING NEXT TO Lisa, an event manager who is wearing a black headset and giving instructions to the control room.

"Dave, put Michelle's presentation on—and make sure the volume is up," she says quietly while looking straight at me. I nod and smile back to let her know I'm ready to go out and CRUSH IT! On the inside, however, I'm sweating, and my heart is racing faster than a cheetah going after a bunny. What a terrible image I just put into your head. Sorry, bunny.

The emcee of the event starts reading my introduction from the stage. "If you've ever wondered what your life would be like if you weren't afraid"—*as she says that, I also wonder what the answer to that question is. I'm VERY nervous to say the least*—"you're about to find out! Welcome Michelle Poler!"

Illustration by ANTONIA FIGUEIREDO/AF.ILLUSTRATIONS

I'm still backstage, praying for my clicker to work but hearing the loud cheers from the crowd reminds me, one more time, that they are not the enemy. There is *nothing* they want more than for me to be EXTRA awesome, so they can go back home and share all about this wonderful speaker who made their trip worth it.

Cue Dave in the control room cranking up the volume—party level—because HERE. I. GO!

I click to my own walk up music—"Dura" by Daddy Yankee (no shame here)—and I start dancing as if I were standing next to Daddy Yankee himself, on stage, at the MTV Video Music Awards. Except that it's just me, in front of eight thousand women whose eyes just popped out real big because they were *not* expecting that kind of dancing at 8:00 a.m. on a Tuesday.

I feel *so* good now. Reggaetón is the only thing that calms my nerves. I'm ready to get vulnerable, share my story of how I was able to overcome my fears and inspire these women to do the same. Because seeing the immediate impact my words have on them is what makes my trips worth it!

But wait! It wasn't always like this! Let's rewind four years back in time:

There I was, taking a shower after a long day at the office, listening to my own playlist "Cool Now" on Spotify, as I always do. The first song that started playing was "I Lived" by OneRepublic. Have you ever heard it? As I was paying close attention to the lyrics, I started crying, well...sobbing. Whatever they were describing in the song, was BEYOND any experiences I'd had. I realized I had *NOT lived*. Well, technically, I'd been alive for twenty-five years, but *living* living...nah. That was the epiphany I needed to say, "Hello, Fears."

It all started when I moved to New York in 2014 to pursue a master's degree in branding at the School of Visual Arts (SVA). Debbie Millman, branding guru and the founder of the program, asked us a *simple* question during the first day of class:

*"Where would you like to be ten years from today?"**

Have you thought about that? A *simple* question—yeah, right. This had to be one of the most daunting questions anyone had ever asked me before in my life.

If you've asked yourself this, you know that when trying to answer you want to dream big...but not too big! You want to sound ambitious but humble. You start dreaming of a 150-foot yacht and somewhere down the line you settle for a freaking kayak! You don't want to disappoint future you with BIG plans that went nowhere and then feel like a big FAILURE, right?

---

* This is a question that Milton Glaser asked Debbie Millman when she was his student.

So, I started to write down semi-ambitious things that I thought could make me happy ten years from that day:

> In ten years, after working for some of the best companies in New York, I will finally become an entrepreneur! I'll be working with Adam, my husband, on building our business together (whatever it is), we will be traveling a lot together for work, and we'll love it, I will be invited to speak at companies and events about my accomplishments, *and* we will buy our first apartment in Manhattan!

Right after writing my plan, Debbie asked us to identify **one crucial obstacle** that could get in the way of our plans. In a matter of seconds, I was transported back to that moment of me weeping in the shower weeks before this assignment was posted. I realized I had not lived because of one thing: FEAR.

Fear was the one obstacle that could totally prevent me from achieving my ten-year plan. How could I apply to the best companies in NYC if I was so afraid of rejection? How could I then become an entrepreneur if I couldn't deal with uncertainty? How could I ever build a thriving business if I was terrified of networking and self-promotion? How would I ever be able to speak at conferences about my "accomplishments" if I was terribly scared of public speaking? And why would we buy an apartment in NYC if I'd been struggling to feel comfortable in this city for the last nine months? I wanted ALL of those things, but I was dreadfully afraid of them.

I realized that **I was hungry for success, but driven by fear.**

The class assignment that came next is what flipped my life upside down.

THE 100-DAY PROJECT

Once the entire class had a clear vision of what our next decade should look like, and had identified the one crucial obstacle that could get in the way of our plans, we had to do something about it, right? We were not just going to stand there and watch our one obstacle ruin our future! That's when Debbie introduced #The100DayProject* to us.

"If you could do ONE thing, repeatedly, for one hundred days in a row, what would you do?" she asked.

One hundred days doing the exact same thing? Talk about commitment! Find one thing that you want to work on in your life and do it for a period of 100 days as a way to improve or become a better version of yourself. I thought of doing:

- 100 days of gratitude
- 100 days of self-love
- 100 days of facing rejection
- 100 days of positivity
- 100 days of journaling
- 100 days of exploring
- 100 days of meditation
- 100 days of photography or ceramics
- 100 days of vulnerability

---

*   #The100DayProject was originally created by Michael Bierut at Yale University.

But, what I ended up doing? 100 days of facing my fears.

In the course of twenty-four hours, I went from a lifetime of "no thanks" to "okay...I'll try." I went from reacting to life, to becoming intentional about life. I went from autopilot mode to **living life to the fullest**.

My goal was to become a braver person but not only for myself. I wanted to become a braver wife for Adam, my husband, and a braver mom for my future kids.

A Little History

I come from a family of World War II survivors; half of my family was killed by the Nazis in concentration camps. My grandparents were lucky—they were able to survive and start a new life from scratch in a different country, Venezuela, where I'm from. The problem is that their fears never went away. In fact, they were carried from generation to generation. My mom was raised with LOTS of fears, and so was I. And while our fears may not overlap, we both had the same attitude toward fear: If it's there, don't bother! When I heard about the #The100DayProject, I immediately knew that this was my one opportunity to break my family's fear chain and redefine my future, which I go into more depth about in Chapter 10. So, please read the first five pages of that last chapter NOW if you want to have a better understanding of where I come from. And then, return to this same page and continue reading!

Despite my family's history, you may be thinking, *How could someone have 100 fears?* It sounds *totally* unrealistic. And you're right! Along the journey I discovered that I didn't have 100 fears, **I only have 7 fears.**

7 Core Fears

It is Day 15 of my 100-day project and as I'm slowly walking from my apartment to the salon, I feel a familiar sensation in my stomach. It's just like the one I experienced on Day 4 when I was about to get my ear pierced.

My feet felt heavier and heavier as I approached the salon. Walking to the salon was not the scary part, and the salon itself was not too scary either. I've been there many times to get my nails and hair done; however, this time it was different. I was going to get the one service I've avoided for the last thirteen years of my life since puberty hit hard: *the Brazilian wax.*

I was terrified, not only of the pain this was going to cause, but the embarrassment of showing my you know what to...*Olga.*

Olga is the Russian lady who was assigned to wax my...yup. And the first thing I asked her was "Do you mind...if I...use my GoPro to film myself as you are waxing me...down there?"

Oh yeah, I not only committed to facing one fear a day, I was also editing one video a day and uploading it to YouTube—which was sometimes scarier than facing the fear itself. Have you ever tried uploading a video of your vulnerable self to the *world wide web* and sharing it with every single person you know? Try doing that 100 times in a row!

That had to be the most awkward question Olga had ever heard! But, God bless her, she said, and I will never forget these words, "Whatever makes you feel comfortable, dear!" You gotta LOVE that woman!

Olga was not only extremely good at her job, but she made my

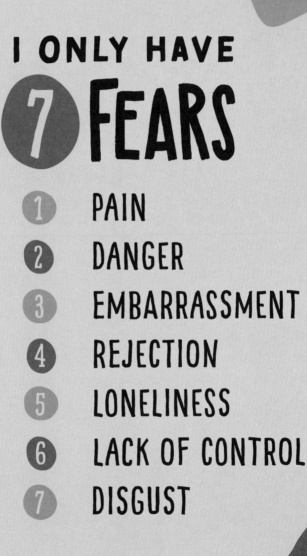

video 10,000 times better. She thought the idea of recording myself was hilarious and decided to be part of the video! She had no idea this was going to be on YouTube, and even less that this video was going to have more than half a million views—maaaaaybe I should've warned her. Truthfully, at that point, it *never* occurred to me that more than a few dozen people were going to watch my videos.

Olga literally showed the green wax to the camera and shared some encouraging words. You might have guessed, it still hurt like hell. Way more than the ear piercing, although that hurt too.

But do you see where I am going here? The wax and the needle were not really my fears. Those were just two expressions of the same fear: pain.

And, just like I was able to draw a parallel there, I started putting together all of my challenges in what ended up being 7 different core fears:

1. Pain

2. Danger

3. Embarrassment

4. Rejection

5. Loneliness

6. Control (or lack of it)

7. Disgust

These 7 fears crystallized by connecting the challenges I was facing with the different feelings they gave me as I was experiencing them, or about to do so.

By categorizing my fears this way, I reached some interesting conclusions. I noticed that I was clearly more uncomfortable with certain categories of fears than with others, and that depending on our personality, our experiences, and our upbringing, we all have our own approaches to each of these categories. For example, I can see how my husband, Adam, is more anxious about the fears that scare me the LEAST and less afraid of the fears that scare me the MOST.

That tells me one important thing: **fear is universal and also extremely personal.** We each have our own comfort zones—we know exactly where they start and where they end, and they are unique to each individual just like your personality or your body is. The things that are uncomfortable to me may be things that you can easily do. For example, while facing my fears of loneliness, pain, and lack of control can tear me apart, Adam would rather face those any time before having to face the fear of embarrassment or rejection.

If you are not sure exactly what I mean by some of these core fears, here are a couple of examples of the things I did that related to each category:

PAIN

I personally have a pretty low threshold when it comes to physical pain; I try to avoid it at all costs. "Girl, you will not be able to EVER give birth like this! I haven't even touched you, and you're already crying!" That is a line I've heard way too many times in my life. At the doctor's office, in the hairstylist's and manicurist's chairs, and now on Olga's waxing table. No wonder I *still* don't have kids!

Some of the challenges I did related to this fear were: eat very spicy food, try acupuncture, walk around New York wearing high heels for an entire day, get my ear pierced, and, well, endure the Brazilian wax you all know way too much about by now (TMI).

DANGER

My project was never about defying death; it was more about living life. So, I tried to avoid doing things that could end up being dangerous or life-threatening. But some of the challenges I faced certainly were pushing that envelope, like: holding a tarantula AND a snake (not simultaneously); jumping from a perfectly good airplane (and then from a cliff); swimming with sharks, visiting a beehive, and the most life-threatening of them all: riding a bike around New York City—don't you DARE deny it, and much less, if you haven't tried it!

EMBARRASSMENT

Some people would rather hang out with bees or sharks before being ridiculed in front of others. But I would rather do stand-up comedy, sing *horribly* in front of a crowd, dance like nobody's watching, and walk around NYC wearing a bikini—in the middle of fall—*before* having to face physical pain in any shape or form. The fear of embarrassment is closely related to our need to fit in, belong, and maintain the status quo—which tremendously limits our authenticity and individuality. If you can relate to this fear, I have four words for you: Chapters 3 and 4.

REJECTION

This one is about emotional pain. Hearing "no" is one of the hardest things humans can face. It causes a deep ache in our hearts. It is what makes us believe *we are NOT enough*. Whether we face rejection from a loved one, a job, a college, an idea, or an investor, that experience can hurt our self-esteem and weaken our confidence—so we try to avoid it as much as possible. Some of the fears that helped me face rejection during the project were: asking strangers for money in the street, going to a networking event by myself, handing out flyers in the subway, applying for jobs at the most competitive companies, bargaining in a street market (which I suck so hard at), and facing trolls online. If facing rejection and criticism is what scares you the most, darling, Chapters 5 and 8 are the ones for you.

LONELINESS

Being by myself is one fear that scares the heck out of me. I would rather spend *hours* with someone I cannot stand than be alone; I kid you not! In order to face this fear and experience what being by myself is all about, I went to the theater, the movies, and even Chinatown by myself—without my phone. The biggest challenge I did related to this fear was traveling solo for a weekend to a new city and exploring every corner by myself. While some people cherish alone time and even consider it necessary to recharge, I dread it.

DISGUST

Just thinking of something that disgusts me is 100 percent outside of my comfort zone and a scenario I would rather dodge altogether. Things that I may find totally disgusting, you may find delicious, fun, or even fascinating. Like eating an oyster, for example. The disgust of eating that slimy sea creature is way outside my comfort zone! Or, going to the restroom at a baseball stadium. Oh, did I say restroom? I meant Porta Potty. And talking about the potty, I changed a poopy diaper of a friend's baby—nasty. And my least favorite, I ate insects. Yup, I ate crunchy crickets. And I used chopsticks, because what else do you use to pick up a salty insect from your plate? You never thought about it, huh?

CONTROL

Raise your hand if you're also a control freak.

Of course you didn't! Because control freaks would *never* deliberately raise their hand in public. Control is the one fear that doesn't allow us to live in the moment, which is why *this* fear is the one I want to tackle first. Before coming face-to-face with the rest of our fears, we have to make the choice to take full advantage of the one life we were given. **The more we try to be in control of our lives, the less we will be able to experience it.**

Some of the challenges that I faced related to control, or better yet, the lack of it, were: crowd surfing at a concert, asking random people to plan my day, walking around NYC blindfolded, riding a mechanical bull, "aging," and becoming an entrepreneur.

Now that you understand the 7 core fears I'm talking about; I want you to rank them according to your personal comfort zone. From 1 to 7, with 1 being *"sure, I can handle it"* and 7 being *"I would rather be dead! See ya!"*

_____ PAIN
_____ DANGER
_____ EMBARRASSMENT
_____ REJECTION
_____ LONELINESS
_____ CONTROL
_____ DISGUST

There is one element that looms over all of these fears like a dark void: the unknown. The truth is that the main reason we fear something we haven't tried before is because we don't know what the outcome will be like. This overlaps with Control (which I touch upon later), but in a broader sense unites all the fears.

The Unknown

Before facing my fears, I used to say I didn't like a bunch of things, but the truth is that I had never even tried them! Once you know what you're getting yourself into, because you've been there before, you can make a decision and define whether you like it. For example, I've dreaded roller coasters since I was a little kid, so for my fear #55 I went to Coney Island and gave an orange, loopy, and pretty fast roller coaster a chance, and...I hated it. Now, I can say that I'm not necessarily afraid of them, I just don't like them.

The opposite happened when I held Honey-Pepper, the tarantula. I thought I was going to die seconds before the animal touched my arm, and then, not only did I survive, I actually enjoyed the experience and even considered getting one for myself. I don't think our current on-the-go kind of lifestyle has room for *any* sort of pet, though I would've totally named her Spanx.

Our comfort zone expands as we face our fears and contracts as we limit ourselves. The problem is that **our ignorance is feeding our fears by the minute!** The only way to know if we like or dislike something is by giving that something a chance. Now, I'm not saying we have to try absolutely *everything*, but if there is something limiting your life in any way, something you've always dreamed of doing, and fear is the reason you haven't tried it, you have got to do something about it. Relax! I'm not throwing a tarantula at you immediately! Keep reading, and little by little, this book will make you realize that the unknown doesn't have to be so scary after all.

To me fear also used to be a sign of something bad approaching. Now I understand that the feeling of fear can also be a sign of growth, progress, and opportunity. I discovered **that the more we say YES to new experiences, the more we allow other emotions to jump in.** Surprise, freedom, curiosity, vulnerability, excitement, trust and connection are a few of the emotions I barely experienced before in my life. My mind used to be so full of fear that I was leaving no space whatsoever for other emotions.

But in order to change our perspective on fear and allow other emotions to jump in, we need to embrace the unknown. Even if that means relinquishing control.

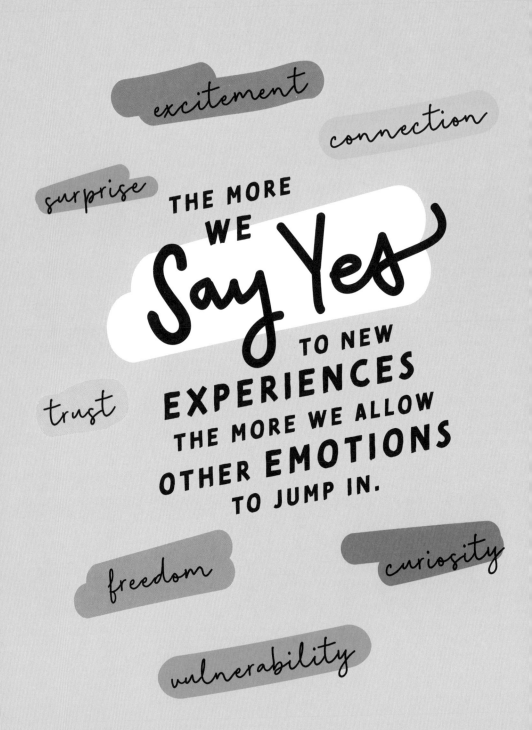

BEING IN CONTROL

What scares us the most about the unknown is the idea of not being in control, and that is the fear I'd like to focus on for the rest of this chapter because it is mainly what was keeping *me* from enjoying my life to the fullest.

Have you ever experienced what *living life to the fullest* feels like?

I can now say that I have, but for the first twenty-five years of my life I never did. Not even on my wedding day. Because without even realizing it, being in control was my priority. To me, being in control meant not leaving things to chance and doing everything in my power to get things to go the way I thought I wanted them to. Always being one step ahead. The problem? **Being one step ahead doesn't allow us to enjoy the present.**

If you are thinking about what to have for dinner while you're having lunch, honey, you're just like me. And sadly, we could be eating the most delicious meal for lunch, but we'll never get to fully enjoy it if dinner is on our minds. And just like that, life passes by and we barely take notice.

"This year went by so fast!" That is a comment I started hearing—*and saying*—more and more often as life progressed. Life used to feel so freaking long when I was a kid, but ever since I graduated from college, years started to fly by. Can you relate to this? If you do, listen up. And if you don't because you are like, twelve years old, hear me out, this will happen to you too (not to scare you or anything, sorry)!

MY OWN THEORY OF TIME

You know how they say that time flies when you're having fun, but a boring day can feel endless? In the very short term, sure. But, in the long run, and based on my own life experience facing fears daily, I came to realize that our brain stores memories in two different ways: singularly and in chunks.

CHUNKS OF MEMORIES: Our brain puts many similar moments of our life together into one single box, making it look like ONE memory! This happens mostly when we have a stable job that requires us to go through the same or similar motions day after day. So, when looking back we only see a couple of "boxes" in there and think: where did the year go?

SINGLE MEMORIES: When we do different things—or, things differently—our brain stores these moments in separate boxes, generating memories that stand by themselves and making time feel *longer*. When we look back and see a bunch of boxes we think: What do you mean it's only March? Feels like October already!

Think about it for a second: try to recall a memory of you sitting at your desk or brushing your teeth in the morning.

Easy, right?

Well, turns out, you are not thinking about *one* specific time when you did that. In fact, you are thinking about all those times when you did the same action. They've been put into *one* memory (one box), which is different from those one-off special moments! Now try to think about a unique experience you had, like your first kiss, the day you gave birth to your first child, or the time you visited Thailand (or any other exciting destination). Probably you can even remember exactly what you were wearing or thinking on those occasions because these memories are self-contained in their OWN box!

As *Scientific American* explains it through the research of Claudia Hammond, British author and presenter, "Our brain encodes new experiences, but not familiar ones, into memory, and our retrospective judgment of time is based on how many new memories we create over a certain period. In other words, the more new memories we build on a weekend, the longer it will seem in hindsight."

This is what happens when we're kids—we are constantly doing new things and discovering life, so time feels longer. And we can also experience this when we go on vacation. Have you ever been in a new city for seemingly fifteen days only to realize that only three days have passed? We explore and do *so* much every single day when we travel, that it is hard to believe it's only been *three* days! #mindblowing

From the time I graduated in 2011 to the day I moved to New York in 2014, I have very few memories. They are all stored in chunks: me at the office, me in my apartment hanging out with Adam, me driving from Point A to Point B in my car singing out loud, me playing with my baby niece, me going out to dinner with my friends at the same spots every time. I just summarized three years of my life in three lines of text; that's a bit sad. Sure, there are a few moments here and there that stand out from those chunks of memories—like my yearly vacation trips, our wedding day, and the night my first niece was born. But, overall, this was my day in, day out, and those three years went by pretty darn fast.

After moving to New York, life started to happen.

I was starting to discover a whole new world filled with new people and countless experiences. There was always something weird (or fascinating) happening on the streets, and I even began to uncover a new sense of self. Epiphany moments just like the one I had in the shower started to happen more and more often, and life started to feel long again, like when I was a kid. A month living in New York City felt like a year because of all the single memories I was accumulating.

It is up to us whether our life feels longer, or flies by before our eyes. And it all connects to how intentional we are in our daily activities and how we must relinquish control in order to immerse ourselves in the experiences that will make our time on earth more memorable, fulfilling, and worth it.

The more we live our life within the confines of our comfort zone, on autopilot mode, the faster our life will pass by. The only way to make it slow down, in the best way possible, is by generating these moments of joy that will stay with us forever. You can create them for yourself and for others as well.

What if you could change up your routine? *Or* better yet, what if you make it part of your routine to do something different every week, if not, every day? For example, what if instead of going to lunch at the same spot with the same people, you decide to sit with a new group of people you've never really interacted with? What if for a change when picking up your kids from school you relinquish control and take them somewhere unexpected and exciting that they suggest instead of to their usual activities? What if you could throw a surprise congratulations party for a friend who accomplished one of her big goals this week? Or plan a last-minute getaway for you and your partner, instead of waiting for him or her to do that for you, like usual?

I know exactly what you're thinking now: *Who has time for that? I don't!* Am I a mind-reader? *Yes!* Okay, no—I'm just painfully aware of the pressures we all are under. But regardless of that, my answer is: **it's not a matter of time, it's a matter of will.** We all have the same number of hours in the day, and for some reason, some people can get more done than others. My ask: stop making excuses related to time, and start being *intentional* about generating these single memories that will last for years and years.

The planning—and fretting about the planning—is secondary to having the ability to immerse ourselves in the experiences and fully enjoy them while they last—which is something that used to be almost impossible for me to do a few years ago. I mean, since you only live once (YOLO), we might as well enjoy our time on earth.

YOLO

Hear me out: **life has an expiration date.** These are 7* things that have helped me LIVE in the moment.

1. Get the Fork Outside of Your Comfort Zone

When we plan experiences that we are comfortable with, and that are repetitious, chances are that (1) they won't be as memorable, and (2) in the midst of them your mind will tune out easily. But, if we plan things that we've never done before, it may not be as comfortable, but I can assure you that (1) you will have a one-of-a-kind experience, and (2) your mind will be so focused on the novelty of this activity, that you will have *no* choice but to tune in.

That is exactly what happened to me during my 100-day project. One day I was rappelling down some rocky mountains in upstate New York, the next day I was learning how to fly a plane, and the day after that I was teaching a Zumba class for the first time to one hundred people in the middle of Sixth Avenue. My mind was in the moment at all times. All of my attention was directed toward the activity that was happening on that day *only*—not on my next challenge, nor on my previous one.

---

*　　I may or may not have a special something with the number 7.

2. Focus on the Road, Forget about the Goal

I have a hard time celebrating my own accomplishments. The truth is that to me life is not about checking things off, it's about the process of getting to that check. In fact, I consider the check the *worst* part. It means the experience is over. I may not celebrate my accomplishments, but I celebrate the daily process.

For example, whenever Adam and I travel for pleasure, we set some goals for the day: visit the museum, tour the market, have a delicious lunch, take a picture with the skyline, ride a bike around the city, and watch a show, all before experiencing the sunset by the mountains.

Adam's approach: Let's take the bus! My research says that's the fastest way to get to the museum.

My approach: Let's walk! That way, we can stop every five steps to take pictures, interact with locals, visit the little shops, buy a few authentic things, try the street food, hop on a tuk-tuk, blah, blah, blah... and if there is still time before the sunset, we can visit the museum!

Maybe that's why we work so well together—opposites attract, they say. I'm not saying my approach is the right approach—no, *obviously* I'm totally saying that. Even Adam, most of the times, thanks me for encouraging him to appreciate the little things along the way and make him see **that the destination is just an excuse to start walking at all.**

This way of approaching life not only works for when we travel, but you can apply this mentality to your job or studies as well. What if instead of getting the job done, we could find joy in the process of making it happen? How much more could we enjoy life that way? One way to change our perspective and feel more grateful about the things we "have" to do, is by rephrasing the task.

Go from "I have to" to "I *get* to," "I *choose* to," or "I'm *blessed* to."

"I have to travel for work" → "I'm blessed to travel for work"

"I have to help my kid with his science project" → "I get to help my kid with his science project"

"I have to plan my partner's birthday" → "I choose to plan my partner's birthday"

Putting it in grateful terms helps us appreciate what we have and find joy in the act of doing, instead of dreading the action and just looking to get it done.

3. Cherish This Time as if It Is the Last Time

"Michelle, what is your REAL biggest fear?"

Toward the end of my project, I started getting that question more and more often. To be completely honest, my biggest fear is losing someone I care about and having to go on with my life—something that took courage to share publicly. As a way to face this fear—without killing my mom or my dad, obviously—I decided to write a *very* honest letter to my parents (who are both alive and in good health). The idea was not only to tell them how much I appreciate them, but also to let them know the things I'd like to change in our relationship to make the best of our time together on earth.

This letter changed my relationship with my parents, and I still can't believe the long-lasting impact that it had. My dad, who had a hard time expressing his feelings with words, became the most loving dad I could ask for. And my mom, who is normally pretty anxious, became significantly more optimistic around me.

If you knew that today was your last day on earth and would be the last time you would experience life as you know it, how would you enjoy every bite differently, every phone call, every cup of coffee, every human interaction, every compliment, every smile, and every opportunity to enjoy today? I know this perspective is super morbid, creepy, and even cliché. But the truth is that we don't really know when our last day or the last day we'll get to hang out with our loved ones will be, so why wait until that happens to cherish every moment, if we could start right now? This mindset helps me be more present and appreciate every little moment, without having to plan or control what comes next.

4. Don't Underestimate Time

Time is the most valuable thing we have, and the one we underestimate the most. Let's say that one day, God forbid, you lose your money. If you work hard enough you will most likely get it back. You can possibly even make more money than what you originally had. There is *no* way to recuperate wasted time. So, in order to fully immerse myself in the present, I take my time seriously, and I don't give it away for free.

Saying *Heck YASSS!* to an opportunity is not the same as saying a tentative *okay* to something you sort of, kind of, maybe want to do. If you spend your days doing those things you sorta want to do, your life will disappear in front of your eyes. Challenge yourself to discover which things, people, and activities make you go Heck YASSSS, and be intentional enough to allocate lots of moments for those.

5. Plan to Enjoy

Remember I mentioned my wedding day earlier, and the fact that I didn't get to enjoy it much? What happened was that while the ceremony and the party were taking place, I was still trying to control things going on around it, instead of immersing myself in the experience. Unless your job is to be an event coordinator, my advice is to focus on doing your best *before* the event takes place, so when the time arrives you can actually be part of the happening. So, instead of overcontrolling things before, *during*, and after every event or activity, next time you plan a gathering with friends, a presentation at work, or your son's birthday party, **plan to enjoy the experience as well.**

6. Live First, Document Later

If you are an oversharer like me, pay attention! I do believe in multitasking, but **sharing** the moment and **living** the moment are two different things that don't go hand in hand. When we're sharing—and I'm talking about social media here—we are focused on giving someone else an experience, someone who is not there with you. Hence, you squander time from your limited-time experience to show others what they're missing. Why do this live—while you are experiencing it—when you can perfectly share afterward? Every time I share my experiences in real time, I regret it. Because (1) I end up missing part of the action and then I'm all like *"wait, what happened?"* and (2) I post in such a hurry that I end up making mistakes or not telling the story correctly.

When I attended the Bruno Mars concert in Vegas, we were asked to put our phones away before entering the venue. We had *no option* but to *lock* our devices in little fabric pouches. Have you ever seen those?

To be honest, at first I was pissed. But as soon as the concert started, Bruno addressed the elephant in the room. He said "I know you guys are mad at me for taking your phones away, I'm sorry! This is *not* my way of keeping this show private. My goal is that you *fully* enjoy the time that we get to spend together during the next couple of hours. I want you to dance and sing with me. I want you to be as present as I am, instead of sharing this experience through your devices with the people back home. Cool? Let's do this!"

I'm can firmly say that it was the best concert I've ever been to precisely because of that. Thank you, Bruno Mars.

7. Do What You Love Like No One's Watching

Have you been in a situation where you have to pretend you're someone you are actually *not,* just because of what people may think of you? You feel completely exhausted by the end, because you were more focused on the reactions of others than on yourself.

I'll tell you about the day I got to experience for the first time for myself and myself alone what living life to the fullest feels like!

It was Day 49 of my project, and a random friend from college whom I hadn't spoken to in years wrote me an email:

Hey Michelle! I'm in New York for one night. I've been following along with your project, and I want to challenge you to go to Times Square tonight and dance ALL OUT in front of everybody. I may join you!

I thought, *Why not?*

I downloaded a song with lots of rhythm and a cool beat and went to Times Square, the most popular, touristy spot in Manhattan. Chris Brinlee, mountain climber and former classmate, was waiting for me in front of the famous M&M's store, ready to enjoy the show. I put on my earphones, turned up the music pretty loud, and started dancing as if I were home in front of my mirror—something I do pretty often. At first, I was about to *die* of embarrassment. People were looking at me as if I was out of my mind, meanwhile Chris was laughing and enjoying the show. So, I continued dancing, pretending no one was watching me, and imagining that I'm in the middle of my own music video. A minute into the song I started to really enjoy the music, the mood, the night, and right then and there, other people started joining me!

Chris couldn't believe it, and his FOMO (fear of missing out) made him join in as well! Before you knew it, this became a party in the middle of Times Square. Even Spider-Man and Elmo joined in! (I would not have been surprised if they were also from Venezuela or Puerto Rico, because they were dancing to my same beat—reggaetón.)

The song ended, and I didn't even notice. We kept dancing for what felt like hours, but it must have been no more than ten minutes. By the end, I felt liberated, and happier than I've ever been. I even thought to myself, *This is what living life to the fullest feels like.*

What I learned that day is that the feeling I experienced only happened because I was able to get over my embarrassment and relinquish control over what other people were thinking about me. I realized that **in order to live life to the fullest, we have to do the things we love like no one's watching.** When we forget that others are watching us and judging us, we do what we do out of *love* and *passion.* Not only will we do a better job, but we will enjoy the moment way more.

I'm not challenging you to dance in the middle of the busiest, most touristy area in your city. But, what is that thing you love to do so much? What if you could do it as if nobody's judging you or watching you? Do you play a sport or an instrument? Do you like to act, dance, or sing? Do you like to paint? To cook? To write? Whatever it is, do it as if nobody's watching. It may require an extra dose of courage, but the satisfaction may even lead you to feel fully alive.

These seven tips helped me be more *present.* Most importantly, **today I can say that I lived.** My hope is that by the end of this book, you can also say that **you lived.** But to do so, you need to be willing to first relinquish control and embark on this very personal journey—which will bring you face-to-face with the unknown, but also face-to-face with a much more fulfilling life.

SCAN ME!

Follow the QR code or go to hellofearsbook.com, where you can find activities that will make this chapter jump off the page.

→ Listen to OneRepublic's Song "I Lived" (it doesn't have to be in the shower, btw).
→ Take a look at my original ten-year plan and the original letter I wrote about my one obstacle.
→ Watch the vlog I made about enjoying life the day my dad's BFF passed.
→ Check out my list with all 100 fears and other awesome 100-day projects I follow.
→ Watch the animation I did about my own theory of time.

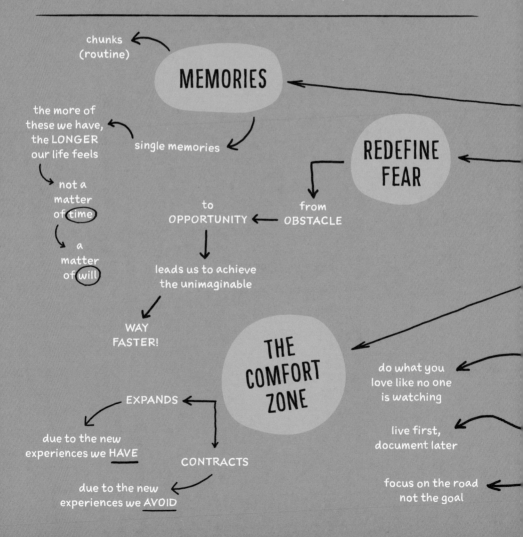

chunks
(routine)

MEMORIES

the more of
these we have,
the LONGER
our life feels

single memories

**REDEFINE
FEAR**

not a
matter
of time

to
OPPORTUNITY ← from
OBSTACLE

a
matter
of will

leads us to achieve
the unimaginable

WAY
FASTER!

**THE
COMFORT
ZONE**

do what you
love like no one
is watching

EXPANDS

live first,
document later

due to the new
experiences we HAVE

CONTRACTS

focus on the road
not the goal

due to the new
experiences we AVOID

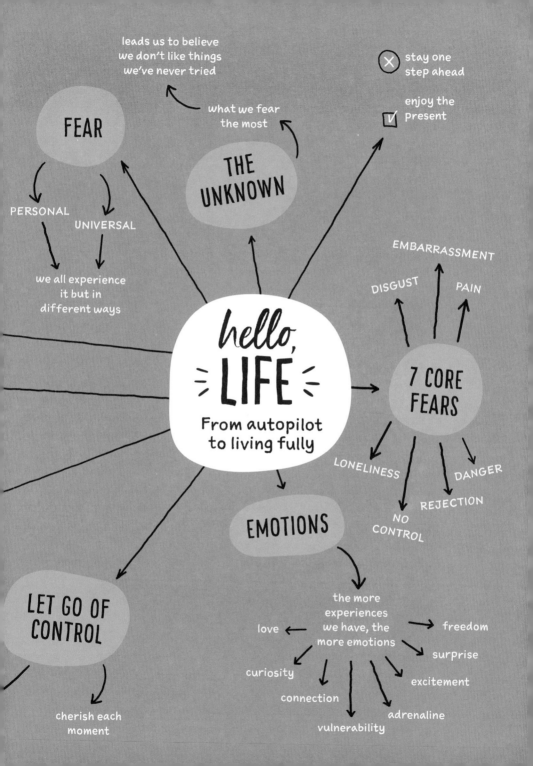

hello, ~~fearless~~ BRAVE

HOW TO INFLUENCE PEOPLE POSITIVELY

IT WAS DAY 95 OF my project—that's how much I was avoiding this particular fear. I rented a car and drove north for about two hours to this awesome water park. My objective was to face the fear I'd been trying to duck for the last twenty-six years of my life: cliff diving.

We got to the park and it was *packed*. Of course, it was the last day the park was going to be open for the season, silly me. Woo-hoo. I packed a swimsuit, three GoPros, and a bag filled with courage. I brought Adam and my friend Tito with me. The idea was to have Tito capture my fall from below while Adam would do so from above.

All my life I've avoided jumping from diving boards or cliffs or riding roller coasters—and don't even get me started about bungee jumping or skydiving (which I also eventually did). Does anyone else here hate that empty feeling in your stomach when free-falling? Yup!

But for my 100-day project, I said I would face ALL the fears that I once avoided, right? This one had to make the cut.

Adam and I climbed up the hill, stood in line, and waited for my turn to jump. Tito positioned himself inside the pool, right below the cliff so he could capture a good shot. Thirty minutes later, I had a line full of kids behind me and a twenty-five-foot fall in front. It was my turn.

"Excuse me, miss, are you jumping or not?"

The lifeguard was getting frustrated by my indecisiveness. I'm almost three times the age of the kids who were in line—kids who were eager to run, jump, and make a splash, and there I was, completely *frozen*. I kept telling my feet to jump, but they wouldn't listen.

Have you ever felt like this, paralyzed by fear? Like you want to take a step, you are 100 percent positive that that is what you have to do, but for some reason you physically can't.

Describing it like this brings me back to my advertising days, when I knew it was time for me to ask my boss for a raise. I remember seeing him in his office, not doing anything too important—all the signs would say **Go, Michelle! Go!**—But I was just too petrified to move into his office...or off this stupid cliff!

I started to let the kids behind me go. I needed more time, or perhaps more courage. But I was not the only one who was suffering: Tito's skin was wrinkling by the second, resembling the aftermath of soaking in the bathtub for more than five songs. He was regretting the moment he thought facing a fear with me would be a *fun* experience.

I turned around and told Adam we should leave. I mean, after successfully facing ninety-four fears, I thought it would be *okay* to say I couldn't face this *one* fear. Think about it: I can say, "I faced the fear of not being able to face one of my fears," right? *Please say yes*, I thought to myself.

"Michelle, we're not leaving! We have three more hours until this park closes. Just jump, please. This is getting a tiny bit embarrassing."

The lifeguard overheard the conversation and added, "Come on, even the little kids are jumping!"

Even the little kids are jumping? Is that meant to inspire me in some way? Those kids may be little, but seeing them jump fearlessly from the cliff does not motivate me one bit.

In that moment, a tiny girl who looked about twelve years old crept to the front to see how high the cliff actually was. She was shivering, all by herself, and clearly having second thoughts. I gave her "the look"—you know, like when you see someone wearing your exact same shoes? We were both petrified and not at all convinced of what was about to happen. *Thank God I'm not the only scaredy-cat in this park!* I thought. *We should just become BFFs and go for cake or do something safer than jumping!*

But a few seconds later, the girl approached the edge again, looked down, closed her eyes, and before I knew it, she jumped! *What the heck?*

Her bravery was just what I needed to face my fear. If she did it, why couldn't I? So, I told Tito to start rolling.

I counted.

1...

2...

I approached the edge...one more time.

3...

Hey, that girl survived. Phew!

4... (sometimes you need 4)

The lifeguard rolled his eyes...one more time.

And

I

jumped.

Did I like it? *Nope.*

Did it hurt? *Very much*—the fall felt so long that at some point mid-air, for some weird reason I thought that maybe I was already drowning, so I had the stupid idea to open my legs to "swim" as I was *still* in the air, and...SPLASH! *ouch*

Do I regret it? How can I? That day I learned a valuable lesson about leadership that determined the way I evolved a personal project into a business and a movement. That day, a random girl taught me how to use my courage to motivate others. That day I learned the important difference between the words *fearless* and *brave*. Welcome to Chapter 2.

FEARLESS VS. BRAVE

FEAR·LESS (adj.)
/ˈfir-ləs/
lacking fear

BRAVE (adj.)
/ˈbrāv/
showing courage

"There comes my fearless friend!" is a line I'm too used to hearing by now. After facing 100 fears, people immediately assume I'M FEARLESS. But every time I hear that greeting I smile (smirk to be precise), and I seamlessly change the conversation topic. On the inside, however, I think of all the fears I'm experiencing at that moment, and I remember how tough it was for me to face 100 challenges a couple of years ago. I shake my head and think, *If only they knew that I am the opposite of fearless.*

A person isn't either fearless or fearful. Fear is one of the things that makes us human. Also, it's what makes us different from each other: while some people seek full-time jobs because they are afraid of independence and instability, others run away from them because of the fear of being tied to one place, one boss, one schedule, and one salary (guilty). Some people love cats, some are *highly allergic* to them (guilty again).

Some fears are there just to protect us. For example, the fear of getting pregnant reminds us to be careful about sex. The fear of embarrassment reminds us to double-check our spelling before sending an important email. The fear of getting sick reminds us to take our vitamins during flu season. They are what keep us safe and on track.

Fear can also be very personal. I recently discovered that some people around me never considered me a fearful person in the first place. In fact, from their perspective I was considered a "brave girl." Turns out that the two people who brought this to my attention suffer from slight social anxiety, and I've always been a social butterfly. As I considered myself a fearful teenager, I had no idea that close friends considered me courageous.

On the other hand, I consider my best friend extremely brave! She willingly divorced her husband to find herself and then she traveled solo all around Europe. For me, the solo traveling would be terrifying in itself. Not to mention the divorce! But for her, it was liberating. Courage is relative!

It's disappointing every time someone uses the word *fearless* to describe me, not only because I know very well that I don't fit the fearless definition, but also because I feel as if **my courage is being underestimated**. I was NOT fearless the day I jumped from the cliff or the time I quit my job or when I delivered my TEDx Talk on Day 100 of the project. Heck, that was BRAVE.

For some reason people tend to confuse the terms fearless and brave, and sadly, they'd rather emphasize *fearless*. Perhaps it is cooler. I sometimes wish I were fearless—my life would be less complicated, plus, I would have fewer stomachaches. But at the end of the day,

Being BRAVE

IS WHEN, DESPITE THE *fear*, WE HAVE THE *courage* TO TAKE *action*, AND THAT IS WAY MORE *powerful* AND *inspiring* THAN BEING FEARLESS.

fearless is an empty word; it means: you're doing the things that don't scare you.

Being brave is when, despite the fear, we have the courage to take action, and that is way more powerful and inspiring than being fearless.

EXERCISE

Have you ever thought about in which areas of your life you would consider yourself to be **fearless**, in which areas you'd say you're **fearful**, and in which ones you're **brave**? Write down some areas of your life for each category.

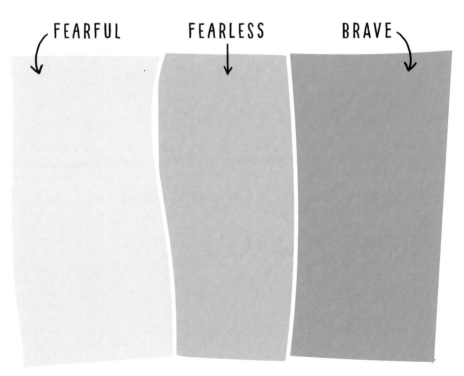

FEARFUL   FEARLESS   BRAVE

Once you enter a few things on this chart, I want you to ask two people who are close to you to help you answer the question above. Ask them in which areas of life they consider you to be fearless, fearful, and brave. Just as my friends considered me brave in the social aspect of life, your friends, mentors, or family members can also have unexpected perceptions of you.

The fearful column should look different once you are done reading this book, of course, only if you are actually willing to put in the work. Because if you would have asked me only a few years ago, I would have told you that I had NO interest whatsoever in facing my own fears. In fact, I grew up thinking that it was okay for girls to have fears and show them in public. While boys...boys were expected to be strong, brave, and tough.

THANK GOD I'M A WOMAN

Almost every single choice I made growing up was fear-based. For example, I would grow apart from friends who owned big dogs and become closer to those who had little fish or turtles as pets. Who am I kidding, *no pets at all* was my secret policy, and it didn't stop there. My fears determined most of the things in my life: from what I'd wear to what I'd eat to where I'd go. I always thought, *If I were a boy, I would've been bullied for being SO fearful. Thank you, God, for making me a girl!*

But did you know that girls and boys have pretty much an equal number of fears? The problem is that society has allowed girls to show their fears in public because of an assumption of female weakness and expects boys to hide them. So, I *never* hid the fact that I was scared of things. Instead of fighting against that stereotype, it was the perfect excuse for me to stay away from uncomfortable situations.

Now I realize that **I was being cowardly and sexist** as a way to shelter myself from the world.

Luckily, things are changing now, and very soon *no* girl should grow up with that kind of mentality. The current feminist movement is empowering girls to be strong, proud, and brave. Advertising campaigns such as Always #LikeAGirl (P&G) or "I Will What I Want" from Under Armour are reinforcing the empowering message that girls are not weak, delicate, or perfect—girls are just as powerful as boys are.

But as women we can't rely on those campaigns alone and get caught up in the messages. We now have the responsibility to not only demand equality but to step up and behave equally; be as strong, tenacious, driven, and courageous as men are expected to be.

Now being a woman means I get to prove the patriarchy wrong, empower other women to succeed, and lead by action. Because being a girl is not an excuse to stay in your comfort zone; it's the reason to get out of it.

My fear now is that in the same way society told boys to be *fearless* ages ago—resulting in men suppressing their feelings and vulnerabilities—some messages out there are now asking the same from girls.

Have you heard about the Fearless Girl statue that was placed on

Wall Street? The one standing up against the famous bull? What an awesome initiative to celebrate International Women's Day and send a message of empowerment to girls out there. But, why call her *fearless*? Is she not afraid to face the giant, iconic bull? Or, is she doing it *despite* her fears?

I mean, think about the girl on the cliff who closed her eyes and jumped anyway. Was she fearless? No! She was HELLA brave, and that's what inspired me to take action.

She didn't push me, warn me about the consequences of not jumping, whisper in my ear an inspirational quote she found on Pinterest, or promise to take me shopping afterwards. She simply jumped.

That girl led by action. She influenced my behavior with her courage.

INFLUENCERS

The other day I was having dinner with my friends, and I said something related to the fact that I'm an influencer. In that moment, a close friend tells me that I cannot simply refer to myself as an influencer, that she doesn't believe that's "right." *Excuse me? Is it wrong to admit one is an influencer? Why is that so taboo?*

An influencer is not necessarily an Instagram celebrity. She is a person who has the ability to **positively influence the behavior or opinions of others**—either online or off-line!

I was not born an influencer. I became one very early in life—before social media was a thing—when I intentionally decided to share my knowledge, thoughts, and ideas as a way to add value and positively impact people around me. If you are also someone who enjoys sharing your tools, tips, knowledge, perspectives, and ways of doing things with others—AND other people follow your advice—then *you,* my friend, are an influencer.

For example, my friend Mauren (yes, the one I mentioned earlier) always tells me where to go and what to do when I travel, and I listen. My brother Daniel is a film director, and he is constantly sharing with me his new tricks to edit engaging videos. And I listen. My aunt Doris loves to share all the tips she's collected on how to live a healthier life. And I listen! These people influence my daily life and make it way better. In fact, they influence me way more than the *real* influencers on social media. This is what I call **everyday leadership**. You don't need to have a certain title, award, or following to be intentional when it comes to influencing those you care about and beyond. But sadly, not everybody is willing to share their knowledge. Some people don't trust their worth—they assume that everybody already knows everything and that their thoughts are not original *enough.*

I have news for you:

The world needs YOUR value. Is it less than perfect? Better yet, did it help you? Then it will help others. Is it about something cliché or already saturated? Read Chapter 4 to learn how to make it YOURS. The truth is that you may not know it all, but I bet you can think of three people who might benefit from your approach. And if three can, three hundred can as well. But the only way to know is by putting your thoughts out there, believing in your worth, and having the best intentions at heart.

That is why influencers are such brave leaders, and I want every person who reads this book to feel like one by the end of it. **If you are a parent, you have the ability to positively influence your children—same if you have friends, siblings, cousins, classmates, teammates, parents, employees, and/or a partner that you love.**

The key? Don't hide your fears nor pretend to be fearless. When you show your true feelings and emotions, you show the REAL you. Being real is what makes you relatable and approachable, and that's why showing courage is way more powerful than portraying a lack of fear. That is what being vulnerable is all about—and it's my personal superpower.

"Without fear there cannot be courage."
—*ERAGON*

The other day, a mom approached me to tell me about her seven-year-old son and his fear of performing in front of the school. She was telling me how disappointed she was when he backed down minutes before the presentation. So, I asked her, "When was the last time your son saw YOU face one of your fears?" A week later she emailed me to let me know that the same day we met, she went to donate blood and took her son with her. He knew how afraid his mom was of needles,

THE WORLD NEEDS YOUR VALUE

and she showed him that she was willing to face her fears for a good cause. A week later, the son had the courage to perform in front of the entire school and made his mom, and himself, really proud.

You can tell others to be courageous, face their fears, and choose growth; you can even try to give them a motivational spiel. But the only thing that will make others reflect on their behavior and consider the possibility of taking action is when they see you face your own fears. The moment you get uncomfortable and start openly facing your challenges, you will see others around you do the same. That is why I created this book—to guide you on that journey of vulnerability, courage, and joy to become the leader you are meant to be.

LEADING A MOVEMENT

The majority of people assume that to be a good leader you must be fearless. In fact, *fearless leadership* is now a trending topic. Companies hire me to talk about it all the time. Sadly, for them, I don't believe in fearless leadership. A fearless leader is reckless. Such leadership is uninspiring, unachievable, and puts the team at risk by setting up others for failure, instead of success. We must be able to understand fear in order to assess risk. I believe in *brave leadership*, the kind that encourages one to take calculated risks informed by what's at stake and thus able to accurately determine if the potential reward outweighs the risk.

Brave leaders are everywhere. That girl on the cliff inspired me to take action, just like I inspired millions when I shared my fear-facing experiences on YouTube. I went from one hundred views to five thousand to five-hundred thousand. Which can mean only one thing: bravery is appreciated. Suddenly, people all over the world started tagging me on videos of themselves facing their fears and thanking me for inspiring them. Who knew that you could have an impact on others just by doing something for yourself? That is how powerful courage can be.

So, I thought: If my stories were able to inspire so many people from different cultures, languages, socio-economic statuses, beliefs, and perspectives, what would the potential multiplier effect be of using my newfound platform to share other people's stories of courage?

That's how Hello Fears was born. It is a social movement where everyday people inspire each other to face their fears and go after the things they want the most.

A movement is not static; it ripples. One story of bravery sparks another that in turn inspires someone else to take action, who now feels empowered to share his or her own story of bravery to hopefully inspire someone else. And the reason why so many people feel drawn to this movement is not because we all have fears, but because we all know that what we want the most is on the other side of that fear, and we want to become brave enough to at least grasp for it.

But who am I to lead a so-called movement?

I'm not a PhD, a therapist, the survivor of a traumatic event, or the CEO of a Fortune 500 company. I'm just a person who decided to go after the things she wanted the most and not let fear get in the way. In fact, "You're such a real person" is the comment I hear most often after my live presentations. I hear it from people of all ages and backgrounds, men and women alike. At first, I was confused by it. *Is that supposed to be a compliment?* Now I understand it is neither good nor bad; it is what makes me relatable, and that is the one thing that makes people think, *If she did it, why can't I?*

Hello Fears is now a community of everyday people inspiring everyday people. So, I want you to be very mindful of the small acts of courage you will undertake as you progress with this book. That is what the next blank page is for! Track your small (and not-so-small) acts of courage. Make sure to flag that page so you can easily return to it and track your progress. By the end of this journey, I'd love for you to share a picture of your list. We will upload it to our platform and share it with the Hello Fears community to inspire others to do the same.

Our vulnerability makes us human; our courage makes us aspirational. But the combination is what makes us genuine leaders—just like the girl on the cliff.

Small (and not-so-small) Acts of Courage

DATE STARTED: /   /

Go to hellofearsbook.com to explore more activities that will make this chapter jump off the page.

→ Watch me jump from a cliff and pretend I was okay.
→ Watch a compilation video of everyday people facing their fears.

→ Go to hellofears.com to read others' stories of courage or share your own.

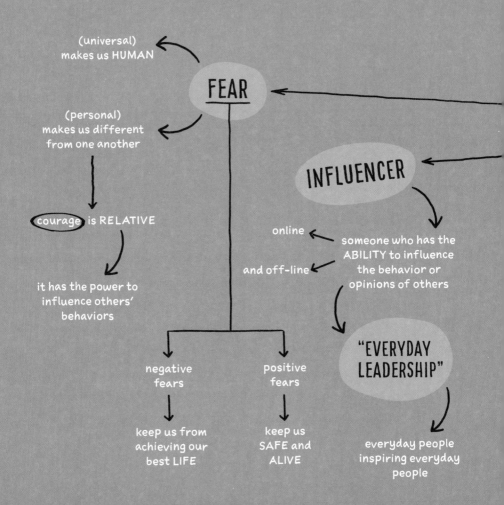

(universal) makes us HUMAN

FEAR

(personal) makes us different from one another

courage is RELATIVE

it has the power to influence others' behaviors

INFLUENCER

online
and off-line

someone who has the ABILITY to influence the behavior or opinions of others

negative fears

positive fears

keep us from achieving our best LIFE

keep us SAFE and ALIVE

"EVERYDAY LEADERSHIP"

everyday people inspiring everyday people

This is an empty word. It means you're doing the things that DON'T scare you.

DESPITE having the fear, we have the COURAGE to take ACTION.

FEARLESS

BRAVE

hello,
~~FEARLESS~~
BRAVE

How to influence people positively

LEADERSHIP

FEARLESS leader
• uninspiring
• reckless
• unachievable

BRAVE leader
• takes smart risks
• knows what's at stake

vulnerable

inspiring

empathetic

genuine

real

human

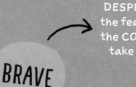

Being a woman is NOT an EXCUSE to stay in the COMFORT ZONE. It's a reason to get out of it.

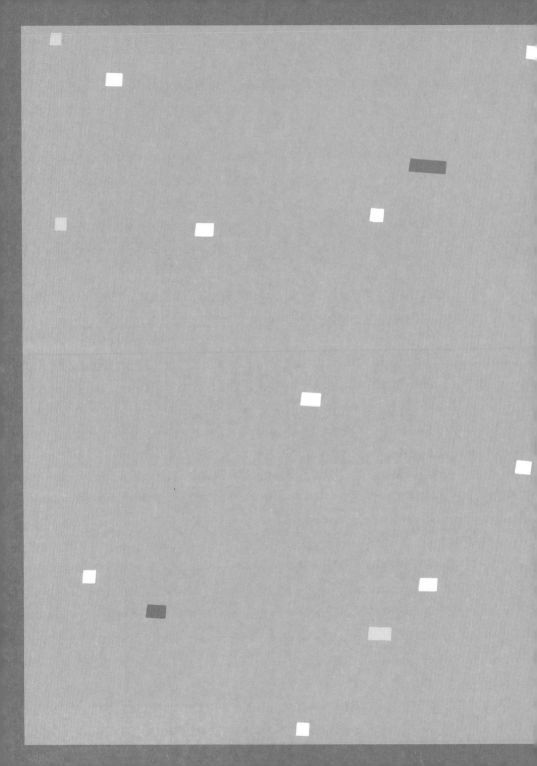

hello, SOCIETY

CHECKING YOUR OWN BOXES

I will kiss a boy when I turn fifteen. I will have my first serious boy-friend at seventeen. I will not have sex before eighteen. I will get married (to the same boyfriend) right after graduating from college. I will find a stable job in my field, work there for a couple of years and then have children when I'm twenty-five or twenty-six...no, twenty-five! We will live happily ever after. End of story.

DID YOU ALSO HAVE A mental checklist with milestones and the appropriate ages for each one? I sure did. And I followed it! Sorta.

Kissing happened at fourteen. Serious boyfriend at seventeen (yas!). And sex, well, at 17.8 (almost!). We got engaged six months before graduating from college and married three months after I turned twenty-three. Phew, I was on track!

Until...January 2012.

Only three months after getting married, I had my first—and thankfully, my last—panic attack. I had no idea what it was at the time. I started experiencing stomachaches, chills, and dizziness, and my heart started racing like never before. My mom was visiting us in Miami, so when she saw me in that state, she immediately knew that I was just having a mild panic attack and helped me calm down.

I had no idea why that was happening, but I had to figure it out! I decided to see a therapist immediately. Luckily, my mom is a therapist, so there was no taboo around therapy in my house. Actually, it seemed kind of like the obvious thing to do at that moment. My mom would always say, "The best gift you can give anyone is therapy." With that in mind, I thought, *Why not?*

Before this incident, I had a very positive experience with therapy at age seven. It's a little embarrassing to admit, but I was still wetting my bed every night. My mom took me to see a therapist who worked her magic and, ta-da, no more embarrassing sleepovers!

Fast forward to 2012, and only a few months into therapy I realized what my problem was: I had accomplished most of the life goals I had on my checklist—all that remained were: buy a home, have kids, have grandkids, and die! And, I was only twenty-three at the time! This realization was shocking. I started to question happiness. I literally had everything I ever wanted: I graduated college with a double major in two fields I was deeply passionate about—graphic design and advertising. I moved to Miami and found a very good job in one of the best advertising agencies there is. I married the love of my life, and I have my closest friends and family nearby. Not to mention the best sushi place was located right below our building. Life was good.

Why, then, was I not 100 percent satisfied with my life? I mean, I finally checked off the boxes that promised lifelong fulfillment and joy.

I started to feel uncomfortable with so much comfort around me. I was only twenty-three and already living such a stable, expected, and monotonous life—one that was not very fulfilling or memorable for me. Something was missing. But what was it? My friends all looked pretty content living their comfortable lives, and it didn't seem like they were questioning it as much as I was. One by one they got married, bought a home, and shortly thereafter, said hello to the little white stick showing a positive sign. I spent a few months asking myself, *Is that what I want?*

That's when it hit me: **most people tend to seek comfort, not happiness**, two things that can get easily confused. For some, comfort is happiness: the more comfortable they are, and the less challenged they feel, the happier they *believe* they are.

Apparently, I am not one of those humans. Who knew?

And yes, having a roof over our heads, loved ones nearby, and enough money to cover our monthly expenses and buy nice things can bring comfort, the kind of comfort we all need and should be grateful for. But that is *not* where I want my life to stop. Because if we would settle for only that, once we achieve that goal, we would stop pursuing our growth path. In other words, settling for the basics would stagnate our human potential.

COMFORT VS. HAPPINESS

That was it. I was not happy. I was comfortable.

I challenge you to circle one of the options below:

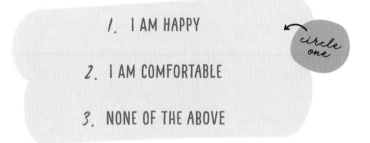

1. I AM HAPPY

2. I AM COMFORTABLE

3. NONE OF THE ABOVE

circle one

Michelle from 2011 would have circled #2 with a pencil. Michelle from 2015 to the present circles #1, using all the colors in the rainbow (and some sparkles).

If you circled #3, it's because you realized you are neither happy nor comfortable with what you have. This book is for you, and I'm glad to have you onboard! Together we'll figure out where your happiness lies and what is holding you back from getting there.

Maybe you circled #2 or #1, but during the course of this chapter and throughout the book you will realize there's room to expand your happiness and/or redefine comfort by facing more fears. Welcome!

This chapter will help you understand where you are, help you move to circling #1, and will add some sparkle to your life in the process.

MORE CHALLENGES = MORE TO LOOK FORWARD TO

My therapist made me realize that I needed more challenges in my life: new goals, new milestones, a purpose other than spending my entire paycheck on stupid things and making lists of baby names. (Chloe is super cute though, just sayin'.)

I came up with a new checklist, just like the one I shared at the beginning of this chapter. But this time, no age limit or deadlines. Most importantly, this list was not influenced by anyone other than myself.

☐ MOVE TO NEW YORK
☐ BECOME AN ENTREPRENEUR
☐ WORK WITH MY HUSBAND
☐ TRAVEL THE WORLD
☐ MAKE A NAME FOR MYSELF

This new checklist challenged me to expand my horizons and gave me hope that one day I could become the successful woman

I'd always envisioned. Paul Arden wrote a book titled *It's Not How Good You Are, It's How Good You Want to Be*—and I wanted to be pretty forking awesome. But I knew it was also going to be pretty forking terrifying.

I had to start somewhere... Hello, New York!

My New York Fears

Getting lost trying to use the subway.

Getting robbed or pickpocketed while on the subway.

Having to survive a snowstorm.

Not being able to fit all my clothes (and winter jackets) in one tiny closet.

The temptation to buy it all—and eat it all.

And most importantly...the competition in the workplace—not being good enough.

It wasn't easy convincing Adam to join me on this adventure. He, being the financial planner of his entire family, thought long and hard before coming to the grisly conclusion that moving to New York was financial suicide.

Adam's New York Fears

Going bankrupt.

Having only one bathroom in the apartment.

It can be really scary to tell your partner you want change, especially when they would also be so integral toward living that dream life, that uncomfortable, challenging, terrifying, but oh-so-very rewarding dream life. So, I laid on the table all the reasons why my happiness and my mental health depended on us moving to New York—*in my most assertive voice possible*. And obviously, he listened, took it seriously and said, "If this is what you need, if deep down in your heart you believe that New York can bring you so much fulfillment and happiness, I'll consider it. But, you will need to prove to me how much you actually want it." Fair.

Adam challenged me to save $10,000. Goodbye shopping, goodbye matcha lattes and Sunday brunch with fluffy eggs Benedicts and mimosas—I was really going to miss that one. I had to start saving all my earnings and prove to Adam and myself that I could make the sacrifices I needed to make in order to reach my goals. Some would call it #adulting. I call it: *In pursuit of my happiness, the heck with comfort.*

This experience taught me that **it's okay to fight for our happiness, prioritize our needs, and find solutions that can satisfy both parties.** It was not about satisfying myself or Adam 100 percent, and it was not about winning either. It was about both of us making sacrifices in order to make each other happy while fulfilling both of our needs. We met in the middle: I saved $10,000, and he said YES to New York!

WHICH **NEED** ARE YOU TRYING TO SATISFY?

(CHECK ONE)

☐ the need to fit in

OR

☐ the need to pursue your own path

EXPECTATIONS

"What do you mean you are moving to New York next year? You've been married for a year already; you're almost twenty-four. Don't you think it's time to think about having a baby and getting a mortgage?"

Those were just a few of the things our friends and family said to us when we shared the news.

Yes, I was expected to stay, to settle, to buy a home, to make little Chloes: according to my mom three is a good number (😔😔😔). But this time I chose NOT to fulfill others' expectations, but instead, to follow my own dreams. Sorry, baby Chloe; you're going to have to wait a little while longer.

I had ambition, and when you're hungry for success, darling, nothing can stop you—not even the idea of going against what others expect of you. **Which need are you trying to satisfy: the need to fit in or the need to pursue your own path?** If you'd rather go for the latter, keep on reading.

Our Needs

Abraham Maslow is the famous psychologist who came up with Maslow's hierarchy of basic needs. *Remember that pyramid?* You probably heard about it in school or college at some point, especially if you majored in marketing, psychology, or sociology. (Nope? Okay, never mind.)

It all starts at the bottom, with our basic needs—air, water, and food (specifically ramen with a soft-boiled egg, if you are like me). On the next level we have our need for shelter, to live somewhere safe and secure, preferably in New York. Just kidding. 😌 From there, it gets way more interesting—if you love to dive into the human mind as much as I do—because right in the middle of the pyramid, Maslow placed our need to BELONG to society in some way or another. And just above that, we have our need to feel good about ourselves, hello, self-esteem! At the very top of the pyramid is the need for self-actualization. This last need ultimately refers to having a higher purpose and tapping into our full potential, which is totally #goals and apparently impossible to *fully* meet. Maaaaybe Gandhi, Oprah, or Malala can tell us what it's like to be so close.

Maslow claimed that our needs motivate us—if we don't satisfy these needs then we can't focus on the higher, more multidimensional, levels. During this chapter, and the next one, we will focus mainly on the middle part of the pyramid. We will analyze and understand why we are so fixated on trying to belong at the expense of focusing on our self-actualization. Because although I agree that needs do motivate us, I have my own theory: **our needs also limit us.**

Fitting In

We're all born with a set of **universal fears** that are tied to our need to survive. It doesn't matter where you're from or how old you are; you are probably afraid of one of the following. In fact, circle the ones you are afraid of!

circle some

TARANTULAS   NEEDLES   HEIGHTS

I just mentally marked all three, btw, so I hope you circled at least *one*! But it's okay! Our universal fears make us human. In fact, you better be afraid of those things because if you're not careful, they can totally kill you. So, go back and circle all three, or don't, you little daredevil.

These fears are part of our prehistoric brain. We are wired to survive, and thanks to this part of the brain, we do! It is instinctive not to touch poisonous creatures, jump off buildings, or walk over sharp objects. The whole point of being placed on earth is to stay alive, and if you're reading this book, it means you are doing one hell of a job at that. Kudos to you and the prehistoric side of your brain!

As we grow, we develop an additional series of fears, the **cultural fears** that revolve around our need for love and belonging. And this set of fears is screwing us up *big time*.

We all have a friend, or two, or three—or we may even be talking about ourselves here—who said YES to a ring because she was too afraid to end up alone surrounded by a bunch of cats (of course, she would *never* admit that). You probably have a coworker who keeps all his ideas to himself because he's afraid of being judged, ignored, or rejected. Or a cousin who never followed her dreams because she was afraid to disappoint her family. What about your best friend, who still swears he's a straight man and is too afraid to celebrate his love for other men?

Our *cultural fears* are getting in the way of really important and overdue conversations.

Every culture has its own set of societal rules and expectations. They are usually written in some form of:

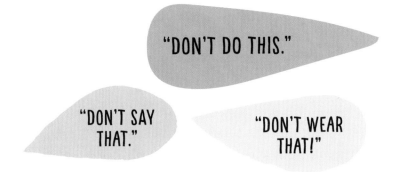

"DON'T DO THIS."

"DON'T SAY THAT."

"DON'T WEAR THAT!"

Or...

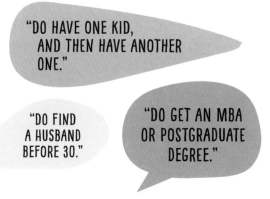

Sound familiar?

Society creates **cultural fears** to make us behave a certain way and shape our personalities to fit its standards. What's interesting is that what may be unacceptable for some, is exactly what is expected from you by others; it all depends on your upbringing:

EXAMPLE #1: While in India eating with your hands is a sign of respect and delight, in the United States it's exactly what can get you kicked out of a restaurant (or your grandma's house).

EXAMPLE #2: In some parts of the United States, women are expected to get married young, be good wives to their husbands, and have plenty of children. However, among professionals in large cities like New York, getting married and having children before the age of thirty is often considered a sign of a career ending.

EXAMPLE #3: While in Latin America, feminine beauty standards are defined by the size of your booty and breasts—and you better have *something* there, otherwise, many think about plastic surgery—in Europe, flat equals sexy, and plastic surgery is a big no-no.

Looks like the definition of perfect or beautiful or successful doesn't have a universal meaning—which means you can dictate it yourself! But wherever we are, the fear of not belonging, or not fitting in, or not being loved or accepted is dictating the majority of the choices we make and the way we present ourselves to others. And I get it, belonging feels good, right? Plus, it is what enables community, family, friendship, and team building. But, if we are not careful, **our need to fit in may hurt our authenticity and our individuality.** It frustrates me to see young people rushing to get married just because they want to adhere to their culture's expectation, or beautiful women going through plastic surgery just because they want to fit their country's beauty standard.

You know what's funny? We don't usually stop to think about the real reasons behind our actions; we go with the flow most of the time. I bet you never caught yourself thinking: *Gee, I should get a mom car so I look like the other moms, and I'm not the weirdo driving the MINI Cooper.* No! You just watch what happens around you, and the need to be and do what others are doing creeps in, and you surrender to it. I was like that too! Hello Tory Burch flats with a huge logo on the front and a crunchy back. You had the same pair? Black? Me too!

Do we really need these things to be happy: a shiny ring, a big wedding, a change of last name, a baby shower and a push present? Have you even asked yourself what is it that YOU want, and then answered that question honestly? Some people do, at fifty! It's called a midlife crisis. It's why your mom got a tattoo and started painting, and your dad decided all of a sudden to visit far-flung places, drive a motorcycle, and wear Hawaiian shirts. Midlife is often when humans start to realize that all the choices they've been making were based on fulfilling others' expectations, and they start wondering about who they really are and what they truly care about. Some never do and spend their entire lives being what society expects them to be—fitting in and criticizing those who don't. My goal is to help you identify who you are TODAY and motivate you to have the courage to live the rest of your life fulfilling your purpose while feeling confident about your true, authentic self. End of rant.

The Difference between Belonging and Fitting In

> True belonging is not passive. It's not fitting in or pretending or selling out because it's safer. It's a practice that requires us to be vulnerable, get uncomfortable, and learn how to be present with people without sacrificing who we are. True belonging is the spiritual practice of believing in and belonging to yourself so deeply that you can share your most authentic self with the world and find sacredness in both being a part of something and standing alone in the wilderness. True belonging doesn't require you to change who you are; it requires you to be who you are.
>
> **—BRENÉ BROWN**

In her book *Braving the Wilderness*, researcher Brené Brown highlights the important difference between **fitting in** and **belonging**. Fitting in is when you adapt yourself to a specific group of people or situation.

Belonging is when you bring yourself, your authentic self, into any group of people or situation. Which phrase best describes your own behavior?

It would have been way easier to stay comfortable, follow the same path as my friends, do exactly what I was expected to do, and make others happy with my choices. But if I would've listened to every person who warned me not to follow my heart, I would've been making choices based on fear: the fear of disappointing others and the fear of not fitting in.

Ambitious, self-driven people like myself don't find anything rewarding in choosing the easier path. If I've learned one thing so far, it's that **making fear-based decisions leads to regret, unhappiness, conformity, and resentment.**

CHOICES

Think about the choices you've made in your life to satisfy others' expectations. Perhaps it was your career choice, the school you graduated from, the person you married (or divorced), the job you go to every day, the number of children you have, the way you look, the city you live in, the car you drive. Which of those choices were made to satisfy you, and which ones were to satisfy others, society perhaps?

List three things about your life that you chose in order to fit in, make someone else happy, or be liked (be as honest as possible with yourself here).

1. _____

_____

2. _____

_____

3. _____

_____

Now, list three things about your life that you chose to make **yourself** happy, even if no one else could ever see that you have or did those things:

1. _____

_____

2. _____

_____

3. _____

_____

The first set of things you wrote above were things you thought you *should* do. The second set of things are the ones you *wanted* to do, so you did them!

Which set of things brings *you* the most fulfillment in your daily life?

The thing is that **the people who tell you to make certain choices won't always be part of the consequences.** Your mom can beg you to have children, but at the end of the day, *you* will be the one waking up at 4:00 a.m. to feed a crying baby. She can try to convince you to study law, but *you* will be the one tasked with understanding the fine print. And she can ask you to dress all ladylike, but it will be *you* who will be nursing your blisters after a whole day of wearing high heels.

From the following list, circle the word that best describes how you feel about certain decisions (if you've already determined some of these possibilities, just ignore or rewrite them; no strict rules here):

1. I want to / should settle in the same city as my family.

2. I want to / should make a name for myself.

3. I want to / should have kids.

4. I want to / should work at a prestigious company.

5. I want to / should discover my passion.

6. I want to / should be my own boss.

7. I want to / should travel to exotic places.

8. I want to / should be an organ donor.

9. I want to / should believe in God.

10. I want to / should _____ .

I'm not saying you must only do the things you want. Every want comes with a set of responsibilities and shoulds. You want to graduate? You *should* do your homework. You want to publish your own book? You *should* start writing. You want to improve your mental health? You *should* go see a therapist! **The ultimate goal of every "should" must be a "want."** If the goal is to fulfill a should for the sake of fulfilling another should (or *someone else's* want), sweetie, you are making your life a living hell.

Go to college because you found a career that sparks your curiosity. Get married because you believe in marriage, and you found the love of your life. Have children only when it makes sense for YOU—not just for your partner. And find a job that brings you fulfillment every day, and if you can't find it, create it. But **never, ever settle**—not for a career, not for a partner, not for a job, not for a city, not for a life that doesn't fulfill you.

The things I value the most in my life are those that I did for myself.

SACRIFICES THAT PAY OFF

I sacrificed a lot to get where I am—but luckily, sacrifices also bring satisfaction. The sacrifice of disappointing society gave me the satisfaction to become my true self. The sacrifice of fighting my fears gave me the satisfaction of changing my career and impacting millions along the way. And the sacrifice of saving $10,000 brought me to New York City. The main thing I sacrificed was my old self, but frankly, I like the person I'm becoming much more. And we will discuss this further in Chapter 9, when we talk about the fear of success.

Now, I want you to take a few minutes to answer the following questions:

1. If you could go back to school and choose a different career, what would you choose?

2. If you could live anywhere in the world, where would it be?

3. If you could surround yourself with anyone in the world, who would you like to surround yourself with?

4. If you could have any job in the world, what would it be?

_____

_____

5. Have any of your answers already come true? If not, what is the very first, tiny step you can take to make some of those dreams a reality? Go back and write that next to your answers.

_____

_____

These are my answers to those four questions:

1. **If you could go back to school and choose a different career, what would you choose?**

I went back to school and got a master's degree in branding after realizing advertising was not really my thing. **Best 👏 decision 👏 of 👏 my 👏 life 👏!** Not only did I confirm branding was my true passion, learn a whole lot of exciting new things, and make amazing friends and connections, but also, my graduate program is where I launched my 100 Days Without Fear project, which completely changed my life.

How did I do it?

I took out a loan that I'm still repaying, I worked full-time throughout the entire year of my program, I stayed in during weekends doing homework, and I stopped eating at restaurants for a year in order to make it happen.

2. **If you could live anywhere in the world, where would it be?**

Exactly where I live today, in Williamsburg, Brooklyn. After dreaming of living in this neighborhood for quite a few years, I made it happen. Why Williamsburg? It has the best of both worlds: the trendy little cafés and restaurants you can find in Manhattan but without the yellow cabs, the buses, the tourists, and the noise. I live two blocks away from the water, the skyline, the bridge, and beautiful parks. My apartment is above an amazing pizza place and in front of an Israeli café, a ramen spot, and the most delicious French bakery.

How did we do it?

Since we travel so much for work, we decided to save on New York rent for an entire year by becoming nomads. We basically lived out of a suitcase staying at my in-laws', my parents', Airbnbs, or even on friend's couches whenever we didn't have clients covering our hotels.

When we returned to New York, we found a one-bedroom in Brooklyn, with one (tiny) bathroom in a not-so-fancy building without a doorman or elevator. It was a small space but filled with lots of good vibes and half of an exposed brick wall (yay!).

3. **If you could surround yourself with anyone in the world, who would you like to surround yourself with?**

Ambitious, self-driven, accomplished people, like my new friends. Friends I handpicked and intentionally invited into my world. Friends who share my same values and have my same level of drive and ambition. Friends who challenge me every day to go further, be the best version of myself, and never settle. Friends who want to see me succeed even when my goals or achievements go beyond their personal comfort zone.

How did I do it?

By reaching out and sending that uncomfortable text: *Hey! I love what you're doing, check out my stuff! You like coffee? I don't, let's get matcha!*

I didn't send those texts when I first launched my 100-day project or when I decided to quit my job to become a keynote speaker. I waited to send those messages. I worked hard AF to become the person who makes myself proud. I accomplished my goals and then set higher goals. That's when I reached out to potential new pals. And when they got back to me, I brought my authentic self into the conversation. I offered help instead of asking for it and started off by perceiving them as people, not as *connections.*

4. **If you could have any job in the world, what would it be?**

I currently have the best job I could ever dream of. I get paid to travel the world, positively impact millions of people, create meaningful content, work with my husband, and be my own boss. Boom.

How did I do it?

I chose to build my own brand while my classmates were applying to the branding jobs I once dreamed about. **I chose** to invest in myself, instead of in a mortgage. **I chose** to expose myself without caring what others might think of me. **I chose** to listen to my heart, instead of other people's concerns. **I chose to choose for myself**, and this is what drives me every single day.

I started checking things off my list the moment I stopped caring about fitting in, because I realized that standing out feels so much better.

And no, I don't have a perfect life and everything figured out, but who would want to have everything figured out, anyway? What's the purpose of living if everything is already in place? What's the satisfaction in that? Plus, you literally can't be 100 percent together, because the moment you get *comfortable* life comes back at you with the most unexpected curveball, and then what? Having things puzzled out is not real; stability is not real. The only thing that is real is your ability to face life's challenges and adversities as they come. Start working on your skills and confidence and stop looking to have things figured out.

EXERCISE

Now, let's go back to the checklist of expectations that began this chapter. Do you remember what that checklist looked like when you were in high school or college? What kinds of dreams did you have for yourself? Did you also attach an age limit to those milestones like I did? Write some of those things here:

My Younger Self Checklist

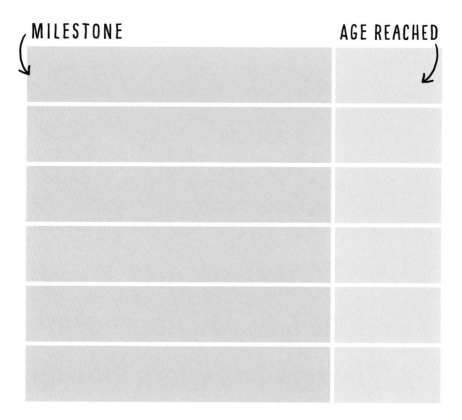

Courage is checking your own boxes—not the ones society expects you to check—and definitely NOT when you are expected to check them.

Taking that into account, I want you to rewrite that checklist, compose a new one from scratch (you can still keep some of those previous milestones in there, don't worry!). This time ask yourself the following question: If I didn't judge my own value according to what

COURAGE *is*

CHECKING YOUR *own* BOXES—
not THE ONES SOCIETY
EXPECTS *you* TO CHECK—AND
DEFINITELY *not* WHEN YOU ARE
EXPECTED TO *check them*.

others expected of me, or if I were unafraid to disappoint others, get rejected, or embarrass myself, what are some of the things I would like to achieve?

My New Checklist

MILESTONE

WHAT'S HOLDING YOU BACK FROM ACHIEVING THESE THINGS?

THREE Key TAKEAWAYS

Go to hellofearsbook.com to explore more activities that will make this chapter jump off the page.

→ Watch my "Moving to NY" video, way before I became a YouTuber.
→ Watch a fun illustrated video that perfectly explains Maslow's theory.

→ Learn more about true belonging with researcher Brené Brown by reading her book *Braving the Wilderness*.
→ Watch me vlog about why we left Miami (a video that summarizes this chapter in four minutes).

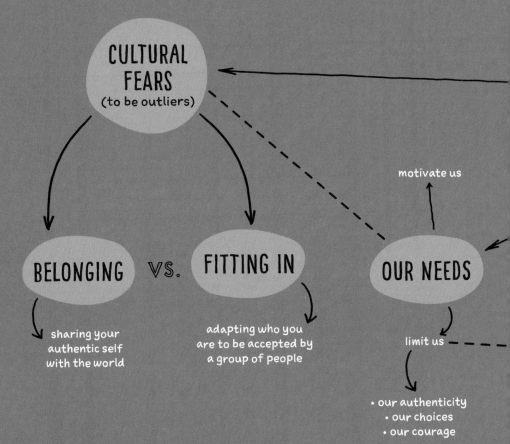

CULTURAL FEARS
(to be outliers)

BELONGING VS. **FITTING IN**

sharing your authentic self with the world

adapting who you are to be accepted by a group of people

OUR NEEDS

motivate us

limit us

• our authenticity
• our choices
• our courage

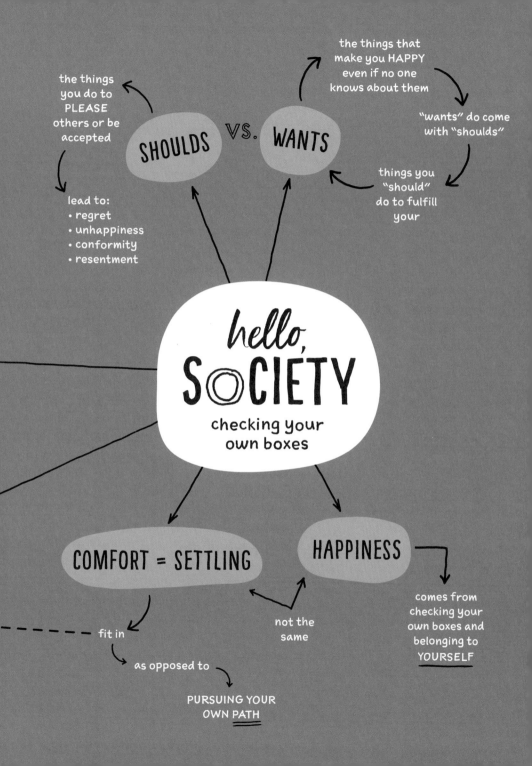

the things you do to PLEASE others or be accepted

lead to:
• regret
• unhappiness
• conformity
• resentment

SHOULDS VS. WANTS

the things that make you HAPPY even if no one knows about them

"wants" do come with "shoulds"

things you "should" do to fulfill your

hello, SOCIETY
checking your own boxes

COMFORT = SETTLING

HAPPINESS

comes from checking your own boxes and belonging to YOURSELF

fit in

not the same

as opposed to

PURSUING YOUR OWN PATH

hello, YOU

BECOMING YOUR AUTHENTIC SELF

"MICHELLE, YOU'RE A PRETTY AMBITIOUS person. My question is: How do you handle yourself when you're not the best at what you do?"

That is a question a Coca-Cola employee asked me after one of my presentations.

I'm already used to the typical questions, like, "Out of the 100 fears you faced, which fear was the hardest one?" or "Did you ever get hurt while facing a fear?" No one had ever asked me about being *imperfect,* so it took me a few seconds to answer, and it probably wasn't the answer they were looking for...

"Now that I think about it, I never, *ever*, aimed to be perfect—at anything I've done in my life! In fact, I'm not a perfectionist AT ALL! I want to be perceived as fresh, unexpected, and memorable, not necessarily as *the best*. Plus, it's all subjective: what's the best for one person could be the absolute *worst* for someone else. Why aim at being the best...if you can aim to be different, to stand out, to be 100 percent yourself? **I would much rather get rejected by others or be frowned upon because I'm different, than be accepted for being exactly the same."**

This chapter is all about becoming your authentic self. It's about not looking around, but looking inside, and then having the courage to turn the inside out. Get ready to get *hella* insightful in this self-branding class you just got yourself into. Welcome to Chapter 4!

MY FIRST FEAR

My will to uncover, embrace, and highlight my authentic self started early in life—which is something I discovered not too long ago when my therapist asked me this sort of uncomfortable question:

"Can you remember a fear you had when you were very little?"

I laughed and said something silly like, "My mom's aunt Silvia, who looked like a clown and smelled like the asparagus she ate three weeks ago. Terrifying!" But she was not joking. I had to time travel to my childhood for this one. She challenged me to go as far back as I could remember, and after a few awkward moments in complete silence, there it was:

"I was about two-and-a-half years old, and I still remember how terrified I was to walk down the aisle—not as the bride, obviously, but as the flower girl."

You would assume that a two-and-a-half-year-old girl would be delighted to wear a big, white, puffy dress, just like the bride's, and make a mess by throwing rose petals everywhere, right?

Illustration by PAOLA ROSALES

Not this flower girl. I was too afraid to walk by myself because I was scared I wouldn't be able to find my mom at the end of the aisle.

From that day onward, I hated weddings. But of course, EVERYBODY wanted me to be their flower girl. So, I purposely sabotaged every single ceremony so no one would ask me again... Muahaha. Sounds devious right? But it never worked, and they kept on inviting me. I mean, I was pretty cute. With those cheeks I could've started my own flower girl business. Just sayin'.

Uncovering this first fear allowed me to understand my behavior throughout my childhood. For the first seven years of my life I was terrified to leave my mom's side at weddings, birthday parties, bar mitzvahs, you name it. A ten-foot-radius circle that surrounded my mom or my dad defined my comfort zone. And I made sure that no matter what I did, I would never go past it—it didn't matter how much ice cream or cake there was on the other side. No amount of sprinkles was going to make me leave that safe zone.

One day, in a desperate attempt to help their shy and highly dependent little girl, my parents decided to seek professional help. They had a hunch that perhaps my shyness was not emotional like they thought. So, they took me to see a bunch of doctors, and...surprise!

I couldn't see! Like, AT ALL! For the longest time they had no clue.

Hello, glasses!

Mystery solved. This seven-year-old girl just needed a pair of pink, round, patterned glasses, and, ta-da! No more problems!

Yeah, right. That was just the beginning of my problems.

I hated those glasses. Not only did I not feel pretty enough when I looked at myself in the mirror, but kids my age started to make fun of me.

Different = Cool

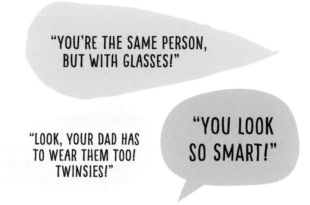

"YOU'RE THE SAME PERSON, BUT WITH GLASSES!"

"LOOK, YOUR DAD HAS TO WEAR THEM TOO! TWINSIES!"

"YOU LOOK SO SMART!"

These are a few of the things my mom told me in efforts to make me feel confident again. But, unfortunately, those words had no effect on me. After all, she is my mom, I mean, she is supposed to say those things and find me cute with or without glasses. Right?

Before giving up, and right when I thought I wanted to be just like everybody else, my mom said something that sparked my curiosity: "It's cool to be different, Michelle."

She explained to me the concept of authenticity—in her own way. She helped me understand that it is up to us to either embrace or despise our "imperfections," and that **when we highlight our authentic selves in a positive light, others will see beauty in us.** She taught me about Frida Kahlo and her bushy eyebrows—*before bushy eyebrows were a thing*—Cindy Crawford and her upper lip mole, and Cher with her deep, masculine voice.

And that, ladies and gents, was my first personal branding lesson.

Pretty soon, I started liking my look, glasses and all. I even made my parents get me a bunch of cheap pairs so I could switch them out and combine them with different outfits. My glasses became my statement piece, and some of my friends even told me they'd wished they'd needed glasses like I did.

As my level of confidence went up, the bullies went away. **Turns out, the more confident you are, the less power the bullies have over you.**

The unconditional love and acceptance my mom gave me made me love and accept myself, but it was her vision that made me change my mind and redefine who I was. She knew what I could become if only I could get over the way I looked. I'm proud of both my mom and my dad for raising me to believe that my talents and personality are more important than my looks and possessions.

So, I made it my mission to always differentiate myself from the rest of the world—not only in the way I looked, but also in the choices I made, the way I behaved, and the things I said. My strategy was simple: look around, notice what everybody else is doing, and do it *your way* unapologetically.

1. When writing my college admissions essay, I decided to be vulnerable and honest. I literally started by writing about how much I don't like to write: "But give me a blank canvas and I will cover it with color; give me a computer with Photoshop and I will make you look like you are in the Bahamas surrounded by a bunch of cats; or give me a Sharpie, and I will illustrate your

next logo." They gave me a scholarship. And I'm writing a book now—since we're talking about writing. 🙌

2. When I quit my job in advertising, I wrote a letter to HR and my team: "It was only when I stopped planning my life and hiding from my fears that I started living to the fullest. I want to face my fear of quitting my job as an art director to finally be happy and free." I published the full letter on my blog along with a YouTube video, and that week I received more than one hundred messages from people who were inspired to change their lives.

3. And finally, when I applied to a very competitive program at the School of Visual Arts in NYC, where only twenty-five people out of one thousand make it, I made a bold move. I sent them my portfolio, but instead of bragging about my work and my accomplishments, I criticized it. One by one. I provided feedback on how ALL of my projects could grow and develop. At the end, I asked them to let me be part of their program so I could learn how to do a better job next time around. I got in!

To stand out, you need to make bold moves, and I would rather **choose bold over bland every single time.**

Now think about a project that you have coming up. Maybe it's an application, a blog post, a resignation letter, your wedding vows, a business pitch, a presentation at school or at work. Whatever it is, how can you make it more YOU? *Different is cool,* remember?

CULTURAL FEARS

Remember those? We literally just talked about them in Chapter 3, so go back if you don't remember or skipped ahead.

Our cultural fears are the ones that respond to our need for love and belonging. In Chapter 3 I talked about how those fears dictate the majority of the choices we make in life—like the job we settle for, the city we live in, and the partner we choose. But this chapter is about how our cultural fears determine the way we present ourselves to the world in terms of our style and personality. Are you being your most authentic self? Or, are you adapting yourself to your surroundings as a way to fit in and feel accepted?

I was able to learn early about the importance of self, cultivate a community around my vision, and go on to build an entire career on these foundations. If you're in the market for professional advice on how to find your own voice and completely own it, you've come to the right place. Let the *slaying* begin!

Your Authentic Self

Do you notice that you act or feel differently when you surround yourself with different groups of people?

ENEMIES

Some people just bring out the worst in me. I notice that when I'm around them my attitude changes, I go from happy, optimistic, and uplifting to pissed and entitled. And I hate that feeling. I know for sure that's not me. At least, it is not the best part of me.

FRENEMIES

These are friends I find cool, but I realize that when I'm around them I feel a certain pressure to show off or appear more confident than I actually am. I get exhausted after a while! And the worst part is, I question my worth constantly when I'm around those people. *Am I worth it? Am I enough?*

FRIENDS

When I'm hanging out with my all-time BFFs or close family members, I feel I can be myself 100 percent of the time, the good and the bad. I don't need to pretend, brag, or hide anything. I know that they know me, the REAL me, and they still like me! Why would I change or pretend to be someone I'm not?

Your authentic self is the person you are when you are by yourself or surrounded by those who bring out the best in you, what I call here your *friends*.

Your authentic self is not the best parts of you; it is ALL of you. It's the perfect combination of all your sides. Take a moment now to think about who your friends are and the person you become when you are around them. That is the real you, and the person I want you to embody 100 percent of the time. Sounds scary? Then we're onto something!

YOUR

Authentic Self

IS NOT THE

BEST PARTS OF YOU;

IT IS ALL OF *you*.

Impostor Syndrome

Comparing ourselves to others is one of the most human things we can do. And it's not even our fault! It starts when we're kids. Our parents compare us to our siblings or cousins from the moment we are born. "Why can't you be more like your sister?" Sound familiar?

Those throwaway statements tell us that we are not good enough in comparison to other people, often people we are supposed to *love*. At school, teachers compare us to our classmates. Through grades we can clearly see we are *better* than some students, but *worse* than others. The problem is that those grades are not taking into account our situation, our struggles, our priorities, or our skills. Grades only portray the results of a very specific system.

As adults, we inevitably measure ourselves in the different areas of life: love, family, career, looks, accomplishments, health, money, happiness...the list goes on and on. We want to know how we measure on the scale of life, and the only way we know how to do that is by comparison. You may be doing better than your cousin but not as good as your best friend.

And that is totally fine. The problem comes when we desire to become someone else instead of the best version of ourselves. When we don't accept who we are or where we stand, impostor syndrome will pop up.

Impostor syndrome is when humans feel as if they are not deserving or good enough for what they have. It is most common among high achievers, and it is a cycle:

"I'M NOT GOOD ENOUGH FOR THIS POSITION; I NEED TO WORK HARDER."

YOU GET A PROMOTION.

"SOONER OR LATER, THEY WILL REALIZE I'M NOT THE RIGHT PERSON FOR THIS ROLE; I'M CLEARLY NOT GOOD ENOUGH. I SHOULD WORK HARDER."

BAM! YOU GET PROMOTED AGAIN.

It doesn't matter how high they climb; they still don't attribute their success to hard work or skills. In this case, they keep getting promoted because they work too hard just to prove that they belong in their current position. But the thought that it was just good luck reinforces their impostor syndrome, resulting in a vicious cycle filled with self-doubt and anxiety.

They say comparison is the main cause of depression. So, **why compare when you can contrast?** That is the key to overcoming impostor syndrome.

COMPARE AND CONTRAST

Contrasting requires vulnerability.
Comparing requires victimization.

When we contrast we must look inside, be okay with who we are, and fully own it. We understand that it is the only way to grow and become our authentic self—even though some people may not like or agree with our choices. But, when we compare, we victimize ourselves, and we allow our circumstances to define us. We focus on our weaknesses instead of celebrating our opportunities.

One thing I learned while studying branding was to look for inspiration in unexpected places. For example, if you are looking to brand a restaurant, don't look for inspiration in the food industry. Instead, think, "If Apple, Netflix, Amazon, or Tesla opened a restaurant, what would it be?" Now, you are comparing your brand to tech, entertainment, and automotive brands, which will help you contrast with and stand out from existing brands in your field. The same principles apply to personal branding.

What is a common trait among the people in your field? What if you decide to ignore it and purposefully do things differently?

Like Stephanie, a family therapist who is revolutionizing her field. Therapists are expected to keep a certain air of mystery around the profession and have strict rules when it comes to their availability. But Stephanie decided to be more approachable than expected by sharing her knowledge of psychology through social media. She is using the Instagram platform to answer people's personal concerns in a way that allows her to bring her expertise to many people and be present for her community daily—not only when she's at her office charging the big bucks. So, instead of limiting her knowledge to her paying clients, she made herself available to the public in pursuit of the greater good through her account @therapyuntangled.

When we look to contrast instead of compare, we get to identify what others are missing. That is known as white space.

OWNING THE WHITE SPACE

White space is untapped territory. It is the thing no one else in your industry is doing—either because they are too worried about fitting in so they haven't seen it, or because they'd rather play it safe and stick to what's proven to work. **White spaces call for courage, authenticity, and vulnerability.** Only the brave ones get to identify them, but most importantly, make good use of them. And taking advantage of them is the best way to disrupt an industry. That's what I did when I decided to switch careers and go from art director to keynote speaker.

When I started my career as a speaker, I was invited to present at one of the largest sports networks during their yearly women's

White spaces call for courage,
authenticity, and vulnerability.

conference. It's a very male-dominated environment, so I was eager to be one of the few woman speakers.

When my agent looked over the agenda for the day, she realized that Carla, vice chairman at a major financial institution and a renowned author, was also a speaker, and she strongly encouraged me to attend Carla's session. Carla is not only a magnificent speaker, but she comes from the corporate world, a world I left and committed to never return to. Since my career change I felt like the happiest human being on earth, but next to Carla I didn't feel confident enough talking to employees about my amazing, new, self-employed life.

There I was, in my seat, listening to Carla and feeling smaller and smaller by the second. I was literally shaking. Yes, it was freezing, but my sweaty palms were clearly indicating that it wasn't because of the cold—but because I was terrified to follow her talk. The more I heard her speak, the more I compared myself to her, until I started to feel like the biggest impostor in the room—hoping not to get caught during my presentation.

Nowhere to hide. It was my turn. So, I did what I do best: dance reggaetón.

Okay, let me fill you in. A few days before the event, Adam challenged me to start that specific presentation dancing reggaetón. Obviously I said NO! I was not going to stand in front of hundreds of people and start dancing all by myself. But he told me I needed to be disruptive, memorable, and brave, and differentiate myself from the get-go. He repeated parts of my presentation back to me, and I had no option but to face my fear and accept the challenge.

I not only danced, I asked people to dance with me. And guess what? No one did. Perfect! Because that was exactly the reaction we were looking for. Now I could talk about the comfort zone and how cozy that feels, like staying in your chair instead of dancing—wink, wink.

I did my best during the forty-five minutes I was on stage, but by the end of it I had literally NO IDEA if my talk was well received or not.

As we were getting in our car to start driving back to New York, we received a text message from the event planner: "Michelle and Adam, would you like to join us during our happy hour event? I'm sure the attendees would love to meet you and ask you a few questions."

Should we continue driving *back* to New York or should we turn around and go to this happy hour event? What would *you* have done?

"Happy hours can be so uncomfortable, you know, having to socialize and make small talk..." Adam said.

"'Do what makes you uncomfortable' is literally a line I said during my presentation," I told Adam. "How on earth are we going to do what makes us comfortable right after I said that?"

I'm so glad we drove back.

That night, *so many* people approached me to thank me. They said that I came across as a real person, which is exactly what inspired them to believe they too could face their fears.

OMG.

For the entire day my impostor syndrome was making me believe I needed to be more like Carla to be appreciated, when in reality I just needed to be myself and own what makes ME authentic.

And there it was, my white space! I heard the comment, "You are such a real person!" enough times to understand that it is one of the things that makes me different from some other speakers they might encounter. Along with the encouragement to embrace their fears, I also gave them a person they could relate to.

So, who is your Carla? Who is that person, or group of people, you are constantly comparing yourself to? The best way to contrast and fight the impostor syndrome is by identifying our white space and owning the things that make us remarkable.

I'M REMARKABLE BECAUSE...

We are constantly taking note of who on our team or in our class is more intelligent, harder working, more good looking, funnier, happier, or wealthier. But the truth is that we can see everybody else's attributes but our own.

WARNING: Uncomfortable exercise ahead. Repeat after me: Bring. It. On.

EXERCISE

I know you love criticizing yourself and finding every possible flaw. I like picking myself apart too. But, for the next five minutes I want you to think *only* about the things that make you *remarkable*. Because the more we look outside and the more we try to be like somebody else, the less authentic we become, and the unhappier we will feel. So, I challenge you to write ten, yes, ten things that make YOU remarkable—not unique, not different or extraordinary. These are things that make you feel proud of yourself daily—like always being on time to meetings or being a good daughter/son or standing up for yourself or being good at recognizing others' virtues. You can include a few of your proudest features or accomplishments in there too. This will be tough, uncomfortable, and very necessary moving forward.

This exercise is a Google initiative, originally created by Anna Vainer and Anna Zapesochini, to empower women and underrepresented groups to celebrate their achievements in the workplace and beyond, thereby breaking modesty norms and glass ceilings. It is meant to highlight to participants the importance of self-promotion in their careers and provide them with the tools to start developing this skill.

I'm remarkable because...

↳

THESE ARE SOME OF MY ANSWERS:

I'm remarkable because I work daily on maintaining a healthy marriage.

I'm remarkable because I love life.

I'm remarkable because I made it in a foreign country.

I'm remarkable because I seek criticism as a way to grow.

I'm remarkable because I accept myself as I am.

Now, once you feel good about your list, ask two or three people who are very close to you to tell you a couple of things that they believe make YOU remarkable—do not share your list with them, at least not before they share their thoughts with you. You may be surprised by their answers.

SELF-ACCEPTANCE VS. SELF-LOVE

SELF-ACCEPTANCE is when we make the decision to embrace those things we can't change about ourselves and that we may not like. Some of the things I wish were different about me are: the fact that I need glasses to see the world, my insane amount of moles and freckles, my low pain threshold, and my short stature. But those things, along with the ones I do like about myself, come together to make me one whole and real person. **Those who get to accept themselves as they are—*perfectly imperfect*—are the ones who are closer to achieving real happiness.**

SELF-LOVE is when you want to become the best version of yourself, so you get uncomfortable to make it happen. You understand that there are things you can't change about yourself, like your voice, your height, your heritage, your sexual orientation, or the color of your skin. But there are other things that you can work on that require a whole lot of self-love to do. If you don't like being a selfish person, you can work on that. If you don't like your negative attitude toward life, you can work on that. You can work on becoming more fit, more mindful, more assertive, and more flexible. It is okay to work on ourselves. **Self-improvement doesn't mean we don't accept who we are; it means we are willing to try to become a little bit better every day.** Also, continuous improvement is what gives us purpose. We hope for a better tomorrow because we know we can control our lives, instead of becoming victims of our current state.

The important thing is that any improvements are for *you*, not for others. If you are okay with your weight, your hair color, or your clothing style, you shouldn't have to change a thing. If you have someone close by constantly telling you that you need to change, you can try to explain to that person that you actually like the way you are and that you hope she or he understands and values that about you. But maybe they just need to change who they hang out with in order to be happier. And trust me, you should too.

In the end, you won't ever make EVERYBODY happy. Start by trying to satisfy yourself, and go from there.

What is one thing about yourself that you're willing to accept? (Self-acceptance)

What is one thing about yourself you'd like to improve in the following months? (Self-love)

SELF-BRANDING

Self-branding is the art of clearly understanding who you already are and having the courage to show it to the world in the most authentic way. Whoever you choose to be, do it proudly, and make sure every aspect of your world resonates with that.

As a way to better understand your personal brand, take this opportunity to look inside and clearly define your values, your tone and your USP—unique selling proposition. These elements will give you a better idea of who your authentic self is and the confidence to embody that person 100 percent of the time.

Values

It all starts here. Our values define what we appreciate and what we believe in. And while we can identify with a million values, each person has about three or four core values that define most of their choices and actions.

Your values not only define a big part of your personality, but they also help you make decisions and prioritize who you're friends with, where you go, and what you wear, listen to, read, or watch. All these things have to align with your core values. If your core value is protecting animals, I seriously hope you are not eating them, wearing them, walking on top of them, or enjoying bullfights on TV.

Some people value family more than others do, some value stability, wealth, or integrity. Looking at my friends and analyzing my relationships with them, what I see is that the friends I'm closest with are the ones who also embody my core values to some degree.

From the moment I first heard about this concept, it took me about *two years* to figure out and clearly define my core values. But after evaluating my decision-making process, I came to the conclusion that even though I value a good number of things, the four core values that determine my actions are:

1. **AUTHENTICITY:** The need to differentiate myself from the rest and be 100 percent "on brand" with myself at all times.

2. **TRANSPARENCY:** The will to be open about who I am and what goes on in my life. This is what makes me a real, relatable, and approachable person.

3. **COURAGE:** The decision to choose growth over comfort every time there's an option, and the determination to get uncomfortable to achieve my goals.

4. **GOOD DESIGN:** Being a designer myself, this value is what makes me want to go to restaurants just because of their logos, their branding, and how photogenic their food looks. It may sound a bit superficial, but I can't deny it; I care too much about design, typography, color, copywriting, and creativity overall.

Your core values can change too! Even though authenticity, transparency, and good design were present in my life from a young age, courage is a value that I intentionally invited into my world only a few years ago. And interestingly enough, it's a value that I never in my entire life thought I could embody. In fact, I'm pretty sure that the value I replaced when I added courage was comfort—two values that simply cannot coexist. You value either comfort or courage.

Now, I want you to circle three values on the next page that are crucial to you. Also, I want you to circle an additional one: an aspirational value, one that you would like to invite into your world. If these preselected values don't resonate with you, make up your own!

VALUES

Accuracy	Authenticity	Adventure	Balance
Simplicity	Collaboration	Connection	Compassion
Courage	Creativity	Discipline	Excellence
Ethics	Faith	Freedom	Friendship
Happiness	Thoughtfulness	Health	Humor
Integrity	Justice	Style	Love
Gratitude	Family	Loyalty	Passion
Power	Security	Stability	Transparency
Wealth	Accountability	Community	Diversity
Equality	Honesty	Empathy	Fun
Inclusivity	Respect	Selflessness	Optimism

Once your core values are in place, you need to define your tone.

Tone

Our tone is what gives personality to our words and actions, and it is a big part of our essence. Imagine the Little Red Riding Hood tale told in the best way by the following personalities:

ELLEN DEGENERES

SACHA BARON COHEN

Julia Child

DONALD TRUMP

What separate approaches—or tones—would these people take that would differentiate their storytelling?

ELLEN would probably be uplifting and sound a little bit like Dory, her character in the movies *Finding Nemo* and *Finding Dory*. She would definitely tell the story with a big smile on her face, even when the hungry wolf is being creepy and scary. I can picture her laughing hysterically at finding the whole scenario a bit ridiculous.

Julia Child would tell the story with such warmth in her voice. Her tone would be soothing and comforting. By the end, we would all be weeping, making sure we learned our lesson and craving one of her delicious apple pies.

SACHA BARON COHEN would probably switch between characters—and hilarious accents—throughout the story. He would embody the wolf, Little Red Riding Hood, *and* the grandma so well without ever breaking character. We, on the other hand, would be peeing in our pants. And the wolf would for sure get that Borat accent he does so well.

DONALD TRUMP would be very monotone, probably repeat each word five times, and ramble a few opinions of his own, including why Little Red Riding Hood should totally build a wall.

How would *you* tell that story? What would your tone be: Comedic, Uplifting, Hopeful, Serious, Technical, Poetic, Confident, Calmed, Innocent, Awkward?

Write down a few words that describe your personal tone here:

_____

_____

_____

_____

_____

Unique Selling Proposition

Your unique selling proposition (USP) is the one thing that sets you apart from the rest, and this is something I learned during my advertising days.

Whenever we were assigned to sell a product or a service, the first thing we had to identify was the USP: What about this product or service does the client want us to highlight?

When talking about Wendy's hamburgers, for example, we would highlight that they are square shaped instead of round. We sometimes would highlight the fact that their meat is always fresh, never frozen. There was always something we could use to appeal to the different audience segments and make Wendy's burgers stand out from other burgers in their category. I still do this now, however, instead of reporting to an external client, I do it for myself and my authentic brand.

What is _my_ USP?

That is a question I started asking myself right after my experience with Carla. I decided to put together a list of the things that made me who I am and helped me stand out from other corporate speakers:

1. Living in the United States, I can say that **I have an accent**; one that people can't really place. Plus, there are not many international keynote speakers, which helps me stand out. And while many presenters are embarrassed to speak with an accent, I'm proud of it. I want to believe it makes me sound a little bit more interesting.*

2. On the same note, I now start and end *all* my presentations **dancing reggaetón**—and showing off my Latin moves (which one day will be featured on *Dancing with the Stars*. A girl can dream, right?). Dancing is a sign of courage, which underscores my message. By the end of my presentation I have everybody shaking their booties, and it is A LOT of fun.

3. Given that I used to be an art director, **I go *all out* when designing my slides,** giving my audience a potent visual experience. This not only helps my presentation be more memorable and surprising, but it also makes it Instagram-friendly. The audience takes pictures of every slide to share with their peers.

---

* I'm talking to you, Ms. Immigrant! Own your background, own your culture, own your accent, and feel proud of it. It's beautiful, and it will help you shine wherever you are.

4. **I look kind of young** to be a keynote speaker, which I emphasize by implementing the concept of **effortless beauty**. I try
hard not to look like I'm trying too hard. I avoid fake eyelashes,
uncomfortable, tight dresses, or shiny heels. I go for a casual but
stylish look.

5. In addition to all those things that certainly help my personal
brand and message feel fresh and real, I have a unique story to
tell that goes beyond the things I've studied or researched. **My
experience facing 100 fears** is something no one can talk about
but me.

Have you thought about what your USP is? If you have more than
one thing, even better! Sometimes it can be a combination of things
that when put together define exactly what makes you different.

For example, if I were to define my USP in one paragraph com-
bining all the elements I named above, I would say: Michelle is an
international keynote speaker with a fresh approach and a unique
story. Her engaging presentation will have the entire room taking
photos of her colorful slides, laughing at her self-deprecating, but
oh-so relatable videos, and taking note of the unexpected life lessons
she shares from the time she decided to turn her life upside down by
going after her fears.

As you can see here, I use very specific adjectives to describe who
I am, what I do, how I do it, and why I do it.

My unique selling proposition is:

Now that you have your personal brand figured out—your values, tone, and USP clearly defined—I ask you: would you have the courage to confidently put yourself out there and let the world know what you are all about?

YOU as a Brand

It's not that I want to turn you into an influencer; okay, maybe I do. But think about it this way: if you were to be a brand, what kind of value would you add to the world? Before answering, DO read this quote from Steven Pressfield from his book *The War of Art*:

Are you a born writer? Were you put on earth to be a painter, a scientist, an apostle of peace? In the end the question can only be answered by action.

Do it or don't do it.

If you were meant to cure cancer or write a symphony or crack cold fusion and you don't do it, you not only hurt yourself, you hurt your children, you hurt me, you hurt the planet.

Creative work is not a selfish act or a bid for attention on the part of the actor. It's a gift to the world and every being in it. Don't cheat us of your contribution. Give us what you've got.

—STEVEN PRESSFIELD

Now, back to you, lovely reader: What is that one thing you are really good at such that others could benefit from your knowledge? If you are a hairstylist, you probably know *a lot* about hair care, which I don't. If you are a nutritionist, you must know all the tips to cook healthier meals—tips I wish I knew. And if you are an OB-GYN, you can share all the fertility advice you've learned over the years—I'm sure many thirty-year-olds who are holding off on having kids (like myself) would love to read what you have to say. At least, I would!

But, would you have the courage to confidently put yourself out there and let others know what you are made of? If I could read your mind at this moment, I'd say you're thinking about the thousands of hairstylists, nutritionists, or OB-GYNs out there, already creating valuable connections and content and being successful at it, right? That's true, but none of them are *you*. None of them have been through YOUR life experiences, have YOUR personality, and have the combination of things YOU bring to the table. And you may not be *the best* one, but you can, *for sure*, share a ton of value in your own voice. It's a matter of storytelling.

Storytelling

My professor at the School of Visual Arts, Dr. Tom Guarriello, shared with us a famous quote from poet Muriel Rukeyser: "The Universe is made of stories, not of atoms." Because the truth is that we can all be saying the same things at the same time, but what will resonate with people is not necessarily the content itself but the way we share it.

Telling your story is the last thing you have to take into account when sharing your most authentic self with the world in your most authentic voice. It's not about *what* you share, it's about *how* you share it. Do you know how many people are *right now* talking about *fear*? Way too many, but none of them discuss it in the exact same way I do.

If I want to inspire you to do a certain thing, for example, have the courage to ask for a promotion at work, I could go straight to the point and list all the reasons why you should do it. Or, I could tell you a compelling *story* of how I did it and then share specific things that helped ME go through with it. This way you have a better chance of getting people to listen, engage with your message, and buy into any idea/product you may be selling.

You could use storytelling in an email to ask for something that you want. You could use it when writing a how-to article for your blog or a post on social media. Or even when trying to sell something on eBay! Don't believe me?

When we moved to New York, we realized we didn't need a car anymore, so Adam decided to sell his beautiful Camaro he loved *oh-so much*. He posted it on eBay with professional photos and a detailed description of the car. Crickets. Nothing happened. There were too many people offering the same car at the same price on that same website.

A month later I asked him to let me try to sell it my way, through storytelling. Out of desperation he accepted my request. I decided to create a fun video telling the story of Adam's love toward his car, showcasing ALL of the good memories we, as a couple, built thanks to it, and how sad he truly was to let it go.

Adam thought this was a terrible strategy because I was showing how MUCH we actually used the car to potential buyers. "Who would want to buy a car that has been given so much use?" Adam asked.

Two hours later, a sixty-five-year-old guy from North Carolina emailed Adam to make an offer. He said:

Adam, I saw your Camaro for sale on eBay. It looks terrific. But I want to add, that I have been so impressed with your wife's video that I have watched it about thirty times so far.

It reminds me of my wife and I early in our marriage when we had a 1967 Camaro convertible purchased as my "graduation gift" from college. It was a huge deal, we were married when I went to school. But like you, life's journey and our growing family meant the convertible had to go.

Watching your video has worked its marketing magic to continue the tradition in the car you are selling. It is a joy to see the two of you enjoying life; much like my wife and I have.

I look forward to hearing from you. Please thank your wife for making some old memories come alive.

There were twenty other Camaros selling for the same price; the buyer chose ours. He and Adam are still good friends today. And I, once again, realized the power in:

- IDENTIFYING A WHITE SPACE.

- CONTRASTING TO DO THINGS OUR OWN WAY.

- USING STORYTELLING TO COMMUNICATE A MESSAGE AND CONNECT WITH OTHER PEOPLE.

- BELIEVING IN OURSELVES AND IN THE THINGS THAT MAKE US REMARKABLE. THE THINGS THAT MAKE US OUR AUTHENTIC SELF!

FOUR Key TAKEAWAYS

Go to hellofearsbook.com to explore more activities that will make this chapter jump off the page.

→ Read my real application letter to Savannah College of Art and Design.

→ Read my resignation letter.

→ Browse my portfolio application to SVA.

→ Listen to a podcast with the awesome Carla Harris.

→ Read Steven Pressfield's book *The War of Art*.

→ Watch a video Google did about the #IAmRemarkable initiative.

→ Listen to my comedian friend Joanna Hausmann talk about self-acceptance on a podcast we did together.

→ Read *Stories That Stick* by Kindra Hall.

→ Watch the video I made to sell Adam's Camaro on eBay.

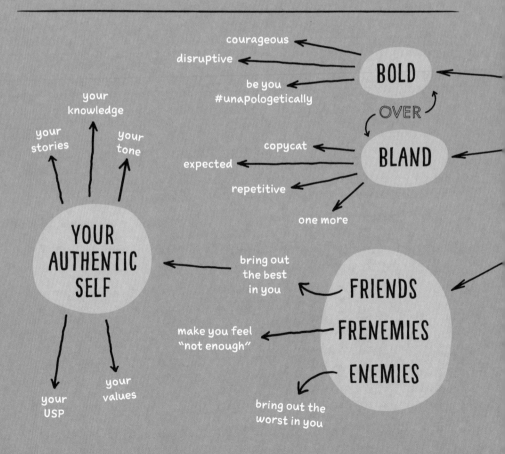

courageous
disruptive
be you #unapologetically

BOLD

OVER

your knowledge
your stories
your tone

copycat
expected
repetitive

BLAND

one more

YOUR AUTHENTIC SELF

bring out the best in you

FRIENDS

FRENEMIES

make you feel "not enough"

your USP
your values

ENEMIES

bring out the worst in you

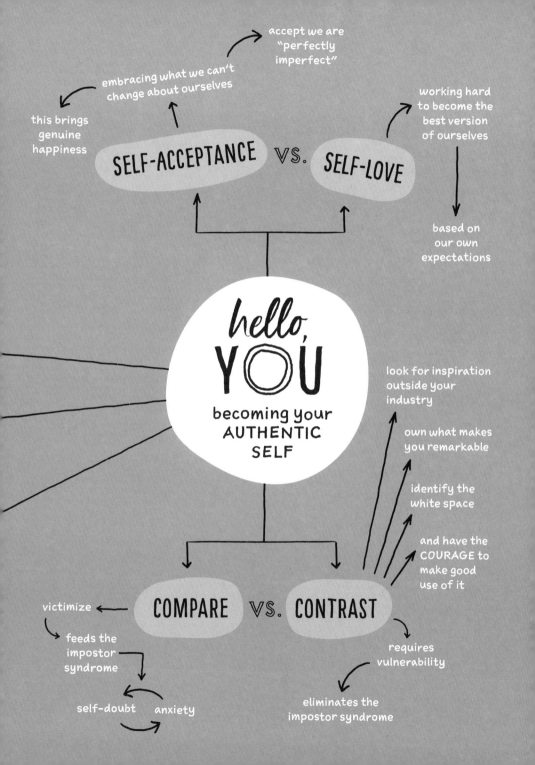

hello, HATERS

EXPOSING YOURSELF AND DEALING WITH CRITICISM

MY WHOLE LIFE I DREAMED about doing something meaningful, so meaningful that even the news would talk about it. I had no idea what that thing was going to be, but it was my personal goal to make it happen before I died.

And that day, I made it happen!

I'm reaching out from DailyMail.com as we absolutely LOVE your '100 days without fear' project—I could do with doing one of those myself! We'd love to write an article about it on the site and I was wondering whether we could use parts of a few of your videos in a montage to run alongside the article (as it's quite integral to the story!) and we can promote it to our millions of world-wide users.

This is (literally) an extract from the email I received on May 19, 2015, from the *Daily Mail*. It was Day 44 of my 100-day project and that day **I faced a fear I had no idea I had: fear of going viral.**

At that moment, I was not afraid, I was just shocked. It was so unexpected that I froze. I didn't know what to say! Hours later my story was not only in one of the UK's most popular publications, the *Daily Mail*, but it was on a few other *dozen* websites.

It was only 9:00 am, and I was *shook.*

I wanted to stay home to process what just happened, but I had to go to work and actually *work*. My boss expected me to deliver a campaign for a supermarket chain and social media posts for a makeup brand. Ugh.

In the meantime, my inbox was being flooded with emails and not exactly those from my boss.

INBOX STATUS: FLOODED

Hey Michelle, I'm Marcin, from Poland. Your story is so inspiring. I wish I could face my fears like you are doing. I've always wanted to travel, but flying terrifies me. Any advice? Here's a suggestion for your next fear: crash a wedding at a fancy hotel in NYC!

My incomplete list of fears was on my website for everyone to see, along with a caption that read, *"I still need more ideas to complete this list; please send your suggestions via email—Thanks!"* My email was out there and people took note. One by one, I started to receive messages from people in different countries saying how inspired they felt after reading my story, and most of them were sharing ideas of known (or their own) fears that I could add to my list. My story and videos were ALL OVER THE WORLD.

Interestingly, one of the fears I was not ready to face was speaking in front of a camera. My videos were all music, text, and wordless facial expressions. And as I read through these emails from inspired people from Brazil to Australia, and Spain to China, I realize this is why people from every country could easily relate and understand. I learned **that the language of fear is universal**; it is an emotion we can all relate to, no matter where you're from, or how old you are.

I know what you're thinking: *What happened to the supermarket campaign and the social media posts that you had to deliver that day?*

I didn't. I couldn't! How could I? All I wanted to do was to freak out in the middle of my crowded office and scream out loud: I WENT VIRAL!!!!

"Michelle, my boyfriend in Spain says that they are talking about you on the radio! He was driving and had to—literally—stop the car to make sure he was not crazy, LOL." I started receiving text messages just like this one from friends all over the world.

Think about it: As I was working on supermarket chains and makeup, my name and my story were being passed around the globe, and it was completely out of my control. What if the same person who reads my makeup post also sees my story shared on the same timeline!

It was 11:00 am, and I still had more than four hundred unread emails from strangers and now about a dozen from my boss—who was NOT happy—wondering where my final files were.

At that point, I started filtering the important emails out so we wouldn't miss those. CNN, HuffPost LIVE, Univision, *CBS Sunday Morning,* Fox News, and Channel One Russia were emailing me requesting live interviews with them, ideally while I was facing one of my next fears.

OMG, OMG, OMG, OMG, OMG, OMG, OMG, OMG.

NORMAL

I always wondered how I would feel seeing myself on the news. It was for sure one of my #lifegoals, but I never really thought it could come true. And when it did, the feeling I got was not what I expected.

I thought that seeing my face ALL OVER would feel:

☐ SURREAL
☐ WEIRD
☐ UNUSUAL
☐ SURPRISING
☐ EXCITING
☐ CONFUSING
☑ ALL OF THE ABOVE

But for some reason it felt... normal.

Normal? Wait, what? Yes. Well, not *normal* normal, but it wasn't as fulfilling as I thought. It felt as if I knew that it was going to happen, or as if I had been there before. I was not surprised nor did I feel weird about seeing my face on all of these amazing websites.

And that made me feel...empty.

I thought, *What the heck? I always wanted this, and now that I have it, I don't even feel special.* Seeing myself plastered everywhere didn't feel fulfilling because I didn't see the impact. It was a one-way street of me TAKING the attention, and that wasn't enough.

But, there was something else that made me feel fulfilled. Reading the emails from people all over the world who could relate to my feeling of fear and wanted my help, was surreal, exciting, surprising, and all of the above. **For the first time, I felt a strange need to help others**. I wanted to answer every single email and say, "I was just like you. Actually, I'm still afraid! But go for it anyway. You deserve to make your dreams a reality, too. I'm here if you need me."

I'm not going to lie, I did enjoy the attention and having the opportunity to face my fears on camera with all the different networks. Doing trapeze with *CBS Sunday Morning,* giving out free hugs in Times Square accompanied by Fox News, and helping people in need with Univision was kind of cool. Seeing my story being shared by celebrities such as Ashton Kutcher, Sofía Vergara, George Takei, Zooey Deschanel, and the rapper Lil Wayne, was *really* cool as well. Ashton freaking Kutcher's social media manager knows my name!

While that was full of buzz and glitz and glamour, realizing that my actions were inspiring others was what really felt eye-opening and impactful. As much as going viral was great, I realized that I wanted to go viral for a **purpose**.

You must be wondering: *What was so scary about going viral, then? Wasn't that something you've always wanted?*

TROLLS

Interesting fact: when you go viral, you not only get love and support like you were hoping. In my innocent world, virality came with *only* praise and recognition. I imagined it was like being on a pink cloud made out of cotton candy...fluffy, sweet, perfect.

Have you heard of trolls? And I don't mean the cute little characters with pink hair from the movie. Trolls are the haters who live on the internet and hide behind a screen to make other people's lives miserable. They are like a stain in the middle of a beautiful white dress: once it's there, it's hard to ignore and focus on the rest of the dress, no matter how beautiful or expensive it may be; the stain becomes your focal point. While my articles on Facebook had hundreds of thousands of likes, and hearts, and positive comments, I would inevitably focus on the mean ones and feel vulnerable, misunderstood, or angry about them.

Youth speaker A'ric Jackson has an interesting definition for *haters*:

H AVING
A TTITUDE
T OWARD
E VERYONE
R EACHING
S UCCESS

Boom.

"Don't focus on that!"; "Ignore the mean comments, Michelle." These were a few of the things my friends were telling me. But, I'm in the fear-facing business now, so **ignoring a fear doesn't seem like the right choice.**

FACING CRITICISM

For one of my YouTube videos (Fear #48, fear of trolls) I decided to print as many of these negative comments as possible and read them one by one in front of the camera. If I was going to face criticism, I had to do it the right way. The idea was to *react* to these comments and show people what criticism is all about.

"She's really quite pathetic having such silly fears in the first place. No wonder she didn't have a proper life until she got over it."

"There are thousands of people conquering their fear every day and you don't see them videotaping themselves, LOL! She just wants publicity!"

"Once upon a time there was a girl… She lived in an effin' cave…"

"Be nice to have the money to do that kind of thing. Or the time. Maybe try 100 days of getting a job."

I had a job! I was working full-time, studying at night, facing 100 fears, and about to go bankrupt. It was just so frustrating, but I didn't know if it was even worth answering these people so they could hear the truth: yes, I was living in an effin' cave my whole life, but that cave was called the comfort zone, and these were legitimate fears that were stopping me from enjoying my life to the fullest.

I simply wanted to become a braver version of myself, for myself, for my husband, and for my future kids.

I realized that the reason why it was so hard to read those comments was because I felt challenged. I guess that in some way, I felt they were right. Up until that point I was facing fears that were maybe 30 percent outside of my comfort zone. But it was time for me to go after bigger, bolder fears, and take this project to the next level. I wanted to prove the haters wrong and show them that this project was for real, that I was for real. Or perhaps, I was just trying to prove to *myself* that I was right.

I took a deep breath and thought: *You think this is a joke? You think*

my fears are silly? You think I'm only doing the things you do daily?
WATCH ME.

That day marked a turning point. I decided to go after my biggest
fears, including:

☐ HOLDING A TARANTULA
☐ QUITTING MY JOB
☐ SKYDIVING
☐ DOING STAND-UP COMEDY
☐ POSING NUDE FOR A DRAWING
CLASS. (I KNOW, KEEP READING.)

Reading the mean comments made me realize it was time to step
it up. I had a bigger responsibility beyond my own bravery. People
were now asking me to face my fears of getting rejected, traveling solo,
being around dogs, and speaking in public, so *they* would be inspired
to do the same.

The haters didn't stop me; they propelled me. They sparked
a fire in me.

This wouldn't have happened if I hadn't exposed myself. That is something I told myself twice. The first time in resentment, as I was reading
the haters' comments online. And the second time in awe, as I was
reading the comments online from those I impacted.

EXPOSED MUCH?

We expose ourselves the moment we put something we create out into the Universe. NOTHING frustrates me more than seeing raw talent hide behind the fear of criticism. I've known amazing singers who would never perform anywhere other than in their shower, when they think their roommate is not home. I've admired talented photographers who conceal their pictures on their external hard drive, writers who hide their journals under their pillows, and grandmas who should have their own Michelin Star sharing their meals only among family.

We don't want to hurt our egos, so no one else needs to know. Right? Because... what if what we do is not good enough? Why do it if there are a few other thousands doing the *same thing*? What if I'm not as good as I think I am? Why bother?

These are the questions that the fear of criticism installs in our heads.

Heck, I question myself every two lines even as I'm writing this book! *What if this book I'm writing is fluff? I mean, I'm no writer, so why would I write something worthy? Another book on fear, woo-hoo. Who would read it anyway?*

But I'm still here, writing it, by myself, word by word, chapter after chapter. I choose to listen to the *other* voice in my head, the one that tells me: *There might be a million books on fear, but none of them in your voice, with the stories only you lived, in your lighthearted tone, and filled with your own lessons and theories. Some people may not like it, but others may love it, and it may even change their perspective on fear. This may not be a bestseller, but what if it's life changing for a few? Keep going, make your future self proud.*

What is the one thing you would share with others if you knew, for sure, that it would be appreciated? What if I told you it could change your life, your career, and your possibilities? Better yet, it could even change others' lives.

Have you seen the movie *Bohemian Rhapsody*? If you haven't, close this book right now, go watch it and come back. SERIOUSLY! But do mark this page so you know where you left off. I've seen it twice. Once in the movie theater, and I cried because Freddie Mercury died. But the second time I cried for a different reason.

As I was watching it, on the plane, I started appreciating the existence of this incredible human being. I could say that his music makes my life a little bit better. And I appreciated knowing the story behind the band Queen and what an idol Freddie Mercury was. And then, I thought: what if Freddie Mercury would've allowed his self-doubt to get in the way? What if he would've listened to that evil voice that we all seem to have in our heads, telling us that we are *not* good *enough*, *not* there yet, *not* good-looking *enough*, or original *enough*. If he would've listened to that voice, *we* wouldn't have had the opportunity to appreciate his talent. No "We Are the Champions," no "Somebody to Love" or "Bohemian Rhapsody"! And then I thought about all the songs that never saw the light of day because of the talented musicians who chose to listen to that evil voice, back down, stay comfortable, and avoid criticism. That's when I started crying.

So, cheers to Freddie Mercury and his refreshing confidence. He put himself out there to be celebrated despite his dad's disapproval and concerns about what society might think about his looks or the people he loved. May we all be a little bit more like Freddie.

BRAVE SOULS

When we dare to expose ourselves, we get *extremely* vulnerable, and that's freaking scary. **To be vulnerable is to be brave.** Because once we take the step, and we are out there, anything can happen: we can triumph or we can fail, but either way, haters gonna hate.

Most of the times we freeze because we get caught up thinking about the backlash or the negative feedback we may get, which would confirm our deepest fear that we are not good enough. But, what we don't realize is that by putting ourselves out there we are already succeeding in the eyes of many—many who would love to have the courage to expose themselves similarly, but haven't. And many who have been in your shoes before and know exactly what you're feeling. I call them the *brave souls*. And if you are reading this book, you're already one of them.

Here's a thought: while haters are going to hate, no matter what, there will be brave souls watching, and they will appreciate your courage, no matter the outcome of your efforts. As a brave soul myself, I can tell you that every time I see someone in the spotlight, sharing their talents with the world, I immediately admire that person. Regardless

to be
VULNERABLE

is to be
BRAVE.

of what that talent is, I see courage, ambition, drive, and guts. My first thought when I see someone else trying to succeed is, "How can I help this remarkable person?" Show me that you care enough to put yourself out there in the arena, and I'll be right there cheering you on!

How can you support other brave souls around you? Can you share or promote what this person is doing? And if it's not quite developed enough, could you offer some advice and encouragement to them to keep trying or perhaps connect that person with the right mentor? Once you expose yourself, the brave souls will take note, and we'll be there to support you. And one day, you will be there for those who are taking their first steps.

And when the brave souls unite, well... Good luck, haters!

Drive attracts drive, and ultimately success will attract success. No one succeeds the first time around. It took me forty fears to be noticed—that is, forty videos that I shot, edited, and posted wondering if anyone cared. Was it luck? Is virality luck? Where does luck comes from? From my experience, luck is what happens when we combine our talents and our courage.

My favorite Broadway musical, *Dear Evan Hansen*, tells the story of a boy who feels unseen, unloved, and like a complete misfit. That is, until one day when he gives a powerful speech in front of the entire school. The speech called "You Will Be Found" goes viral, and in the play, millions of teens around the world finally felt seen, understood, and not so lonely after all. At some point, Evan, overwhelmed by the amount of views and positive comments, asks, "What happened?" and his friend answers, "You did!"

It was not Evan's talent that put him on the map, it was his courage to be seen, to stand in front of others and share his powerful speech.

The truth is that **you will only be found if you make yourself visible.**

FOUND

But what happens when you are actually found? What if your project, idea, or song becomes a hit? You thought it was going to be tough to get noticed? Get ready for what happens next!

"Of course, she had it easy; her parents supported her." Or, "Look at her, she only got there because of her looks." Or, "With that kind of money, anyone could have done it." There is nothing an envious person likes more than to sabotage others' success.

It is easy to explain others' success when we bring external factors into the equation and blame those for the outcome. It makes some people feel better on the inside, like they would have also been capable of the same thing if only they had the same starting conditions.

It is difficult for some critics to go beyond the easy excuses and understand that often the only reason that person got where she did is because she worked damn hard to be there. Hard work can take us anywhere, but we have to be willing to get *consistently uncomfortable* to make it happen, and only some people are willing to go there.

But, regardless of what you did, or didn't do, in order to be found, people will judge.

Being Judged

Here's a great case in point:

The other day my friend called me and told me about a conversation she had with her aunt. First let me tell you this: my friend's aunt has never spoken to me in my life. She knows who I am, I know who she is, but every time I see her around and smile at her—meaning, "Hey! You're my friend's aunt!"—she ignores me and looks away. How rude!

My friend's aunt told her, "Probably the reason why your friend Michelle is not having children, after six years of marriage, is because she can't. That simple. Poor thing, she must be devastated."

My friend insisted that that was *not* the case. She told her aunt about my success, which she knew about, and tried to explain to her that kids were the LAST thing on my mind. But it was pointless. Her aunt kept on insisting that *not being able to get pregnant was what was happening to me and that I was too ashamed to admit it.* It was the most comfortable explanation for my predicament. God forbid it was my choice at the time. I was a nomad at that moment in life, traveling from one place to the other and enjoying my life to the fullest with my hubby at twenty-nine years old.

When my friend told me about the discussion, I was only thinking about one thing: content! This was the perfect story to share with my online community and highlight an important message that could potentially help others in the same kind of situation.

While I'm being judged for not having children after six or seven years of marriage, other people are being judged by their families and peers for living with their partners without having a signed document, or for choosing an unexpected career, or for dressing in a certain way. We are all expected to conform. But when we do *not* conform, we give gossipy people reasons to talk about us. Some even may blame our success on situations they can disapprove of or that we might have no control over (and therefore can take no credit for).

But we must do what feels right *for us* and be confident in the decisions we're making—our happiness depends on it.

> "Don't apologize for evolving past
> someone else's comfort zone."
> —SOURCE UNKNOWN

That is the quote that helped me get over those who judge me simply because of the need to feel good about themselves and their narrow assumptions. **We cannot allow the haters to define us or get in the way of our success.** But we must not ignore their comments either.

My Strategy for Managing Criticism

These are four things I like to do when I hear people judging or criticizing my actions:

LISTEN: First I listen to what they have to say and pay close attention to the words they use to talk about my life, my choices, my projects, or me. Some assumptions will be downright ridiculous, but others may help us understand that we are not perfect. There is always room for improvement, and considering these unsolicited suggestions is when we get the most vulnerable. Is this true? I ask myself. It is important to be very honest with ourselves when trying to answer this question.

I try to leave my initial rage aside—trust me, no one likes to hear criticism—and I answer that question without fooling myself. Even when the comment is coming from a negative place, it is important to define what percentage of it is actually true.

CREATE DISTANCE: I think for a moment about the person expressing the opinion. Where do they come from? What kind of work do they do? What kinds of choices have they made? What kinds of struggles, if any, have defined their life? What is the intention behind the comment: is this person giving me constructive criticism because they want the best for me? Or are they trying to make me feel unworthy so they can feel better about themselves?

This information will allow me to better understand where the comment comes from, and it will help me create a healthy distance between me and the words spoken. I'm less likely to take it personally when I understand the context.

MAKE A CHOICE: Will I listen and change the way I do things based on this comment? Or, will I keep doing the things I'm doing because I believe so much in myself that I can't wait to prove this person wrong? Either way, the answer I choose has to be a growth-based decision, not a fear- or comfort-based one. If I decide to change, it would not be in order to please others or avoid further criticism; it would be because I recognize that I can do a better job and that even though this comment may be hurtful, it comes from an honest place. But, if I decide to keep pushing in the same direction, it's not because I'm stubborn or comfortable but because I trust that I'm secure in my hustle and doing the best that I can to achieve the results I desire.

TAKE ACTION: Use criticism relentlessly as fuel to become an even better version of yourself and prove those who doubted you wrong—and yourself right.

In my case, after hearing my friend's aunt's thoughts, I took action by sharing this story on Instagram with my audience, and the response was overwhelmingly positive. Hundreds of people wrote back sharing their personal stories of the times that they've been judged and the times they said, "Thanks, but no thanks."

But while listening to other people criticize what we do can be hurtful, our worst critic lives with us, inside our head.

MY (POSING NUDE) EPIPHANY

One day, as I was in the middle of my 100-day project, one of my good friends visited me in New York. As I faced my fear of changing a poopy diaper (using her six-month-old daughter as a prop), she challenged me to do something I would've never thought myself capable of: "Hey, what about posing nude for an art class?"

I freaked out (to put it mildly). I told her she was being irrational and even doubted if we were truly friends. I mean, who would say that? But it didn't take long for me to realize that my reaction was a clear sign that I was afraid to accept this challenge. Afraid? I was terrified!

I kind of hated her a little bit for putting that thought into my mind. That was a fear I never thought about facing, not even when I was in art school drawing other people naked. But it was too late; the idea was out there, and I couldn't ignore it or pretend I didn't hear it.

It was the morning of Day #77 of my project, and to prepare, I did something I deeply regretted: I got a Brazilian wax (Fear #15 all over again) with Olga, the same person who helped me face my fear the first time around.

It was a beautiful July afternoon when I arrived at the New York Academy of Art. I begged Adam to come with me to help me with the video, but he said—and I still find it hard to believe—"Are you kidding? I'm even more scared and uncomfortable than you are." With Adam sitting this one out, I went *all by myself*, and upon arrival the art teacher showed me the way to the changing room, which was basically just an empty classroom.

The teacher asked me to get undressed and walk over to the next room where the students were waiting for me. You know the feeling you get when you get undressed at a doctor's office? It was like that, but eighty-four times worse. I turned on my camera and while standing off-screen started taking off my clothes piece by piece—yes, including ALL of my underwear—and showing item after item to the camera from the side. Happily, I took a big enough scarf to wear as a robe as I walked from the changing room to the actual classroom.

When I entered the room, I saw something that made me regret the Brazilian wax I had gotten hours ago and the no-carb diet I had done that day. The two people that were modeling before me had beautiful curves—plenty of curves—interesting body shapes, and hair everywhere—lots of it. That's when it hit me: art students are not looking for what the media defines as *perfect* bodies; on the contrary, they want enough *material* to work with. Crap! What was I thinking? Suddenly, being hairless and skinny sounded like a terrible idea. I felt ashamed and silly for doing what I did.

This was the drill: I had fifteen minutes to strike five different poses.

There I was, standing in front of a dozen people I've never seen in my life wearing ONLY my scarf when the art teacher asked me to start. In that moment I was so lost and confused that my first reaction was to turn around and face the wall. I just couldn't face the students as I was dropping my scarf on the floor.

Three minutes was enough time to have an epiphany. While I was power posing and giving my bare back to the students, I understood that this wasn't about me, like *at all*. The students were not there to judge the models. They were there to fulfill *their* mission: to create beautiful art inspired by *whoever* posed for them. They weren't looking for one specific body type, texture, or color; their job was to use what was in front of them to put all of their skills into practice and make precious art. That thought made me feel like such a FOOL. I was so nervous about exposing my body and being judged that I never, for one second, stopped to think about the students and their needs.

This thought helped me get through the full fifteen minutes and make the most of my time there. Instead of hiding my insecurities, I decided to highlight them: I bent my body in weird ways to create shadows and interesting shapes. I let my tummy go. I owned my moles, freckles, and stretch marks, and I got creative in order to give them *good* material to work with.

Once the fifteen minutes were up, the entire class started clapping. They all knew I was facing my fear and were able to see my evolution from Pose #1 to Pose #5. I felt by the end like they were proud of the way I approached it, and that left me with a feeling of deep accomplishment.

But what happened right before I left shook me the most.

After getting dressed again, I came back into the room to see the drawings, and I couldn't believe what I saw. While I was so worried about showing my body, there was one guy who spent the entire class drawing...my face.

This experience made me realize that while other people do judge, **no one is judging us the way that we judge ourselves.** Even when we judge others, we are indirectly saying something about who we are, not about the person who we are judging.

My best friend's aunt was not talking about me; she was talking about herself. Maybe she had problems getting pregnant and that's the reason it took *her* a while to have children. Or maybe her world is so small that women are only supposed to give birth to kids, not to books, successful careers, or self-sustained marriages.

When trolls online were saying that my project was not inspiring, they were talking about themselves, spending hours on Facebook watching video after video, posting negative thought after negative thought, instead of daring to go out there, defy the status quo, and make something out of their time on earth—something a little bit more inspiring than criticizing strangers online.

Think about those who have criticized you in the past. Think about what their words may be saying about them. Also, think about the things you've criticized about others. What is that saying about you?

I have three requests for you right now:

REQUEST #1: If you don't enjoy being judged or having people commenting on your choices behind your back, don't do it to others. Easier said than done, right?

Talking about others behind their backs is so natural that we don't even think about it; we just do it. It is the most satisfying conversation topic; I mean, why talk about our own insecurities if we can talk about others'? I'm guilty of this too, big time. I love gossiping, but I try to reflect on my words and change my conversation topic more often than not. The next time you catch yourself talking about another person behind their back, change the conversation.

REQUEST #2: If you feel strongly about a choice someone you care about is making, have the courage to say it to their face. Many people would rather keep their opinions to themselves to avoid confrontation, but sometimes we need people to tell us what we are doing wrong in order to change. What ultimately matters is that you have good intentions at heart. Trust your intuition and dare to have the difficult conversation. I personally value my friends who tell me the things I'm doing wrong more than the ones who outwardly agree with everything that I do. And as much as it makes me uncomfortable to be honest with others, I do it as often as possible.

REQUEST #3: Be gentle with yourself. Protect your ego instead of crushing it. This is something I've become really good at as I've learned how to distance myself from internal as well as external criticism.

When I was starting my career as a speaker, I had the opportunity to speak at two awesome events one right after the other. HUGE mistake. The problem was that they were completely different.

One event was on August 30 at a girls' school in Palo Alto. It was my dream to speak at girls' schools, and this was my one chance to do it right. I wanted to wow the principal of the school so she would recommend me to other girls' schools around the country. It was going to be my first time ever speaking to youth, so I had to craft an entirely fresh new talk for that age range (11–18)!

Soon after, I landed a gig at NETFLIX for August 31. (!!!!) And it was only blocks away from the school where I was going to speak the previous day. Was it a coincidence? I believe it was destiny.

During our prep call, the client was very specific about their objectives. I had to recreate my corporate talk to please this audience. It was a great challenge that was going to make my corporate presentation better anyway. So, I accepted their request.

Basically, I had to deliver two NEW talks one after the other. Two talks I cared *a lot* about.

Months before, when I accepted both events, Adam warned me NOT to do both talks so close to each other. He asked me to postpone the Netflix talk so I could have more time to prepare. I was so excited about the opportunity to speak at such a remarkable company that I didn't listen. I didn't want to ruin my chances of speaking there, so I accepted their terms.

But what ended up happening is that I focused so much on nailing the girls' talk the day before, that my Netflix talk went horribly wrong. I screwed up.

On August 31 at 1:00 p.m., as I got into the car I rented to drive back to the airport, I didn't need to hear "I told you so." I was disappointed in myself, frustrated, and simply ashamed—even more so when I watched the video of the presentation and realized that I kept confusing the words *fearless* and *fearful*. OMG, *major* shame! At one point I even said, "New York is not for the fearless." What?

After going through such a sour moment at Netflix's HQ, I promised myself: (1) to not leave so little time to prepare before an important event and (2) to never again confuse the word *fearful* with the word *fearless*.

That could've been a crappy day because of what happened. I could've spent hours giving myself a hard time and looping in my head the things I said wrong. But instead, this is how I handled my own internal critic:

I accepted my mistake without giving myself a hard time.

I took note of all the things I could improve before giving my next presentation.

I turned the page as quickly as possible, instead of staying stuck overanalyzing what I said or did wrong.

I forgave myself.

I practiced gratitude for the lessons learned.

Internal criticism can be devastating if we allow it to be. You could either take it as: *I'm clearly not good enough.* Or, you could flip it around and think, *There is ALWAYS room for improvement. At least I know now what to work on.*

★ **Remind yourself that you did your best with the knowledge and tools you had at the time.**

On a podcast interview I recorded with my friend Odette Cressler, she shared a fantastic tool to deal with internal criticism. Turns out, she gave her ego-crushing-self a nickname; in her case, she called her Odelia. Now every time she catches herself practicing negative self-talk, she is able to distance herself from that mean voice in her head. She refers to Odelia as an outsider with the worst possible intentions. Odelia is not there to help or give constructive criticism, she is there only to harm and destroy.

Odette is not Odelia, and it is her job to push aside the interloper instead of listening to what she has to say. This is her way of dealing with internal criticism.

If you would have to assign a name to your inner troll, what would it be?

THE UNIVERSE

Days before virality hit like a tornado, I had a conversation with Adam, during which we seriously considered giving up on the 100-day project.

We were funding the project ourselves, and it was getting out of hand. We were trying to keep up with the New York lifestyle and also pay for my master's degree. It was just too much to cover. We thought about getting to Fear #50 and continuing the other half in the future.

After going viral, my YouTube channel went from eighty-nine subscribers to twelve thousand, and views went up from four thousand to four million. That was enough to ask companies to sponsor the more expensive experiences we wanted to tackle: skydiving, zip-lining, shark diving, plane piloting, and taking on water parks, camping sites, and car rentals. Everybody wanted in! They were excited to give us their best service for free in exchange for having their logo on my next video and being seen by thousands of subscribers. Not one dime more had to be invested from our pocket into this project—pretty awesome, right?

For me, this was a clear sign. The universe wanted me to keep facing my fears and inspiring millions. And if trolls were the price I had to pay to accomplish what I did, so be it. I'd pay that price anytime. Wouldn't you?

I call it speaking the language of the universe.

The universe does not always respond to prayers; it responds to positive action. You want something? Prove it. That's how I see it. The more uncomfortable you get, the more the universe listens.

If haters and criticism are stopping you from achieving your dream, it's time to get uncomfortable and say: BRING IT ON!

FIVE Key TAKEAWAYS

Go to hellofearsbook.com to explore more activities that will make this chapter jump off the page.

→ Watch the video of me reading out loud all the MEAN comments left for me online.

→ Listen to "You Will Be Found" (lyrics by Benj Pasek and Justin Paul) from the musical *Dear Evan Hansen*.

→ Watch an inspiring talk about working hard by Vanessa Van Edwards at World Domination Summit.

→ Watch the film *Bohemian Rhapsody*, or listen to any Queen album to be as inspired by Freddie Mercury as I am.

→ Watch me face my fear of posing nude in front of an art class.

→ Listen to a podcast episode with Odette/Odelia.

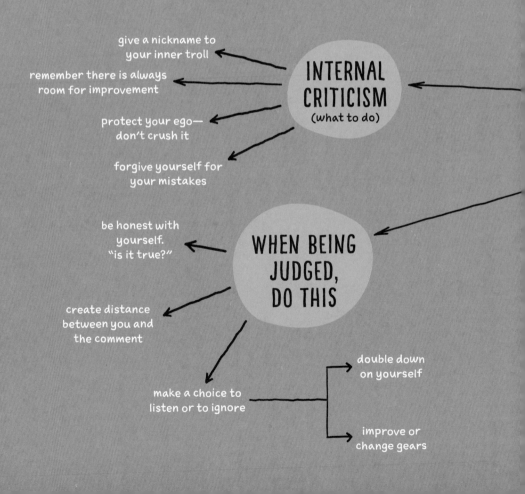

give a nickname to your inner troll

remember there is always room for improvement

protect your ego—don't crush it

forgive yourself for your mistakes

INTERNAL CRITICISM
(what to do)

be honest with yourself. "is it true?"

create distance between you and the comment

WHEN BEING JUDGED, DO THIS

make a choice to listen or to ignore

double down on yourself

improve or change gears

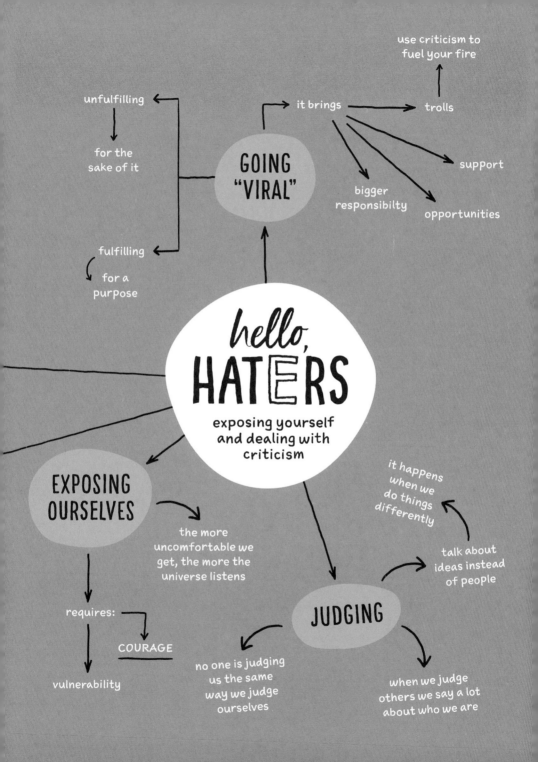

hello, EGO

UNLEARNING FAILURE

IN NOVEMBER 2016, I HAD the opportunity to speak at one of my favorite companies at the time: Facebook. During the Q&A session, one of the employees asked me a question that left me puzzled for weeks. She said, "Michelle, since you talk so much about failure, tell us about a time that you failed. What did you learn from that experience?"

Fail? Seconds that felt like minutes went by, and I couldn't come up with an answer even if my life depended on it. Finally, I decided to be honest—and told her that I just couldn't think of anything—which kind of felt like admitting a small failure, after all. But I promised her that I was going to reflect and get back to her.

I realized that the reason why I hadn't failed up until that point was because since finishing my 100-day project I was not allowing myself to go big. I was so comfortable traveling and speaking that I was not building anything new. I had hundreds of ideas, but I was not willing to execute. There was always a good excuse for delaying my plans.

In December 2016, I made a promise to myself: If I come up with an idea and my immediate thought is, "No way, it will never work out, I'll totally fail," I will do it, no questions asked! Technically my 2017 New Year's resolution was: *to fail*. And that's exactly what I did. **I turned my fear of failure into my goal.**

If failing is also one of your biggest fears, welcome to Chapter 6! This chapter will help you change your perception of "failure," strengthen your ego, and empower you to **choose action over perfection.** But first, let's understand what the heck defines failure.

#FAIL

Imagine you are in the middle of a big waiting room. You are surrounded by all sorts of doors, but only one of them will take you to the place you'd love to go. The doors have no signs, so there could be anything behind them.

This is not the typical waiting room. This room is familiar; it has some nice couches, Netflix on the TV, Wi-Fi, AC (that only you can control), good phone reception, coffee, pizza, cookie dough ice cream, I mean, what else do you need!? A puppy? Okay, yes, it also has a puppy.

It's even connected to your friends' and family's waiting rooms, and they can come and go as they please—better yet, as YOU please. They are all in their own cozy waiting rooms, surrounded by unopened doors. They seem happy, or at least, at ease.

Behind those doors is the unknown.

You hear tales of failure, rejection, heartbreaks, setbacks, and challenges from those who have tried opening them; challenges that you're not sure you could handle.

But behind one of those doors lies success, YOUR kind of success, whatever it is. The one thing you've always dreamed of becoming is right there, behind one of those doors. But, which one?

Give yourself a minute to envision what is behind the winning door. If you could dream of having your ideal lifestyle tomorrow, what would it look like? What things would you like to have? Who would you like to be surrounded with? How would you like to be perceived by others? Go ahead and write or draw everything you envision on the next page. Treat this space like your own vision board.

The only way to find out which door leads to your dream is by taking the risk to start opening some of those doors.

Most people choose to stay in the waiting room. I mean, why risk it? Why go through all that hassle, pain, and discomfort if nothing can assure you that you will ever find the right door? You

MY VISION BOARD:

FAILING *is not* THE ACT OF GETTING IT *wrong,* IT'S THE ACT OF NOT EVEN *trying* AT ALL.

look around, and you realize that you're surrounded by people who have never opened a single door and still had a decent life. So, why bother?

I have bad and good news for you:

Bad News

The door you're looking for will never be the first one you go through. Like it or not, you will have to go through multiple doors before you find the one you want. For some people it may take just a few doors, but for others more than expected.

Good News (1/4)

One thing is for sure, every single door you open, good or bad, will get you closer to the right door. Every door will have a purpose. Each one will have something to teach you. Plus, you will know which door *not* to open next time around, since you already know what's behind it! Every door is a step closer to your success.

Good News (2/4)

Every door you open will change you. Since you will have learned different lessons and been exposed to new perspectives from the different doors, you will not be the same person after opening them, therefore your waiting room will not be the same either. Things you enjoyed doing before may now seem like a waste of time, and ideas you thought were crazy may not sound that crazy anymore. The more doors you open, the more your worldview expands and evolves.

Good News (3/4)

The life you want is there, behind one of the doors. And the cool thing is that NO ONE can take it away from you. Only you have the right combination to open that door. So, you are not competing against anyone but yourself. The faster you take action and start opening those doors, the sooner you will get to the right one.

Good News (4/4)

The right door will not be your final destination. Instead, it will lead you to the opportunity of a lifetime, and if you take it, it will offer a new set of doors just for you—doors you had NO IDEA existed.

———

All these doors and waiting rooms are making me feel pretty Nietzsche-like right now. I mean, where the heck did that come from? Am I like a total philosopher and had no idea? That'd be kinda cool and very unexpected.

Aristotle or not, though, I hope the message was crystal clear:

Life is full of opportunities, and since we cannot (yet) predict the future, we can't possibly know which opportunity will be the right one or how to take full advantage of it. But, as long as we wait for things to happen to us, doors to open by themselves, or someone to guide us and tell us where to go, we might as well be waiting forever, in the comfy waiting room of life.

Taking our chances can lead to failure, rejection, and emotional pain.

But, when you know where you want to go, and you are committed to getting there, nothing else is as important. And suddenly **failing is not the act of getting it wrong, it's the act of not even trying at all.**

A door can come in the shape of an email, the email that can bring you funding for your upcoming venture. It could be the person sitting right next to you on the plane who can become your next partner, coach, or sponsor, if only you would initiate a conversation. A door can be you signing up for a dating app, where you may meet the right one after knocking on multiple doors and having the patience to explore what's behind them. It can come in the shape of a question posed in class that you courageously decided to answer, taking the risk of being wrong and feeling embarrassed, but also of being right and impressing your classmates and professor.

Not everybody wants to leave their comfort zone and go after big things. But every time we hold ourselves back from taking a risk, trying new things, or venturing into the unknown we are one step further from achieving our goals. When we prevent failure, we are also preventing success. That simple.

If I've learned one thing, it is that **the real enemy of success is NOT failure; it is actually comfort.**

COMFORT

It's what keeps us from innovating or from raising our hand to suggest the next big idea. It convinces us to stay with people we no longer love and at jobs or in positions or cities that can no longer nourish our growth. Comfort begs us to watch one more episode, instead of facing the blank canvas on our blog. And it is what makes us stay in our cozy waiting room, with all the doors shut.

Comfort tells us things like, "Good things come to those who wait." But who reading this book is tired of waiting? I know I was.

I realized this in 2013 when I went to the movie theater to watch *Jobs*. I got home late that night and as I was thinking about the movie plot, I started crying. I was COL—*crying out loud*—because I wanted to be someone and make a dent in the world, just like Steve Jobs. The problem was that I was not even close.

My actions were not leading me to dent the world in any way other than selling a few extra Wendy's burgers through radio or TV commercials. My daily existence was about fulfilling someone else's dream, not my own. Perhaps my boss's dream of winning a Cannes Lion Award with one of those creative radio spots. Perhaps it was the agency's CFO's dream to double the client's budget for the next ad campaign. Or maybe, Wendy's CMO's dream to sell more burgers. For sure, I was not working toward my dream. I guess I was too comfortable working for others, being told what to do, and having a steady paycheck. *Keep doing what you're doing girl, you're doing just fine! Why risk what you have now?* my superego would say.

> "People of accomplishment rarely sat back and let things happen to them. They went out and happened to things."
> —LEONARDO DA VINCI

I needed to find my growth path and take bigger risks to get there. That is when the idea of moving to New York popped into my head. That was my first step toward *happening to things*—which is a concept I now implement toward every goal or dream I add to my bucket list. If I really, really want something, I go and GRAB it—Gary Vee would be SO proud of me for saying that. You don't know who Gary Vee is? Gary Vaynerchuk?*

What is the first step, or better yet, the first door you should try to open in order to achieve your desired lifestyle and the success you envision for yourself?

Remember this when answering the question:

> "Doubt kills more dreams
> than failure ever will."
> —SUZY KASSEM

The first door I will open is:

Hey, I'm not saying this will be the right door. You may totally get it wrong. Just like Steve Jobs totally got it wrong when he recruited

---

* Seriously? Shut up!

John Sculley as the CEO of Apple, which later backfired and left Jobs without a job—pun intended. And he still made it, because he kept on trying, he kept on learning from his mistakes, and most importantly, he never allowed the fear of failure to get in the way of success. One thing I know for sure: once you open that door you will be one step closer to *happening to things.*

This takes us to a very important set of fears—the personal fears.

PERSONAL FEARS

We don't take care of many things in our life as much as we take care of our self-esteem. I mean, if we protected our bodies as much as we did our egos, dental hygienists would go out of business, rates of skin cancer would drop, and we would all be in perfect shape. But it's not the case. In fact, we go to great extents to prevent failure and rejection, because no real pain hurts as much as emotional pain.

Every day millions of people settle for jobs that give them enough to feed their families but too little to feed their souls. Many settle for a husband or a wife, instead of looking for the right *partner* who supports their dreams and makes them part of his or hers. Others settle for a lifestyle that may be convenient, but not fulfilling. And while in Chapter 3, I talked about how most people settle as a way to be accepted and easily belong in society, this time I'm talking about settling because it would be just too hard to knock on the wrong door and hurt our ego.

According to Freud, our psyche is divided into three parts (and this totally blew my mind): the id, the superego and the ego.

The **id** refers to our instincts, those signs our mind sends to our body without much rational explanation. Like when we feel like eating a piece of delicious cake we see on the menu or buying a pair of shoes that are way outside our budget, or even when we feel a desire to kiss someone who looks attractive. Those are impulses that we constantly need to control or limit; otherwise, we would live in complete anarchy, and everybody would do exactly what they feel like doing in the moment without taking into account the consequences of their actions.

On the contrary, the **superego** is heavily influenced by external factors: our parents, teachers, friends, and community. Our superego is the ideal image that society put into our heads, all those expectations we feel pressure to meet. We are expected to behave well, be kind, be successful, have money, have a stable relationship, procreate, celebrate certain holidays, and believe in certain things.

Our **ego** is the one stuck dealing with our id and our superego. It's like the middle brother trying to satisfy everyone in a way such that no one gets hurt—not too much *pleasure* and not too much *pressure*. Your ego's job is to find balance and make the best choices according to your priorities and goals.

The biggest threat to our success is when our ego is not strong enough to keep our "superego" under control. We have so much pressure (internal and/or external) to appear as though we are okay at all times, that we'd rather not take the risk. Because when we set extremely high expectations for ourselves, and we live unquestionably by those expectations, we don't allow room for error. But the thing is, our errors can teach us the most valuable lessons and give us the impulse to move forward.

On the other hand, when our id is out of control, we may take too many risks, but not in the smartest way. Such an approach can lead to failure after failure and eventually to frustration and low self-esteem.

People with strong egos are capable of dealing with their id's impulses and their superego's requests to maintain the status quo and still dare to take smart risks.

Choosing to see failure as a lesson is a choice, one we can get in the habit of making, but only if we are willing to work hard enough on redefining ourselves in the face of failure over and over again. This is a quality of those who I consider to be *doers*.

DREAMERS AND DOERS

Dreamers are those who love to plan their *perfect future lives.* They can spend hours brainstorming and scribbling plans in their colorful dotted journals. They have pages filled with brilliant ideas, action steps, and rough, but promising, sketches. They have all the motivation, but also, all the excuses not to execute *yet!*

Doers not only come up with dope ideas, but they also execute them instead of waiting for others to make them happen. They don't believe in excuses or wait for the perfect moment. They know there is no such thing. They believe in the art of trying and failing, and trying again.

What differentiates dreamers from doers? You guessed it: **courage.**

Personally, I like to surround myself with doers. They motivate me to **spend less time dreaming and more time building.** And don't get me wrong, dreaming big was the first step to getting where I am today, so by all means *dream,* but it is doing that made my dream a reality.

The first time I thought about this concept was when I met social media and marketing guru Verónica Ruiz del Vizo. After *stalking* her for weeks on Instagram, she accepted my invitation to go for coffee and talk about possible collaborations. As soon as I shook her hand, I noticed that she had a tattoo on each wrist. One said *Dreamer* and the other said *Doer.* She told me that she realized she needed to become both a *dreamer* and a *doer* in order to live the life she envisioned for herself. And this woman was not kidding.

the **REAL ENEMY** of **SUCCESS** is **NOT FAILURE;** it is **ACTUALLY** **COMFORT.**

As our conversation progressed, I remember she asked me about my plans and goals. While I was sharing some of my ideas, her consistent answer was, "Cool, so you did that already?" And I would be like, "No! It's just an idea I have..." This back-and-forth happened about *four* times. And by the end of our meeting, I realized that I was full of unexecuted ideas.

As our friendship progressed, and we went from "a nice contact to have" to F *R *I *E *N *D *S,* I started to be more and more motivated by her accomplishments and her attitude toward life. Just by watching her fulfill her goals, I felt challenged—in the BEST way possible—to take action on my personal dreams. And for that I'll be forever grateful. Now it's ME who asks fellow dreamers, "So when is that idea rolling out?"

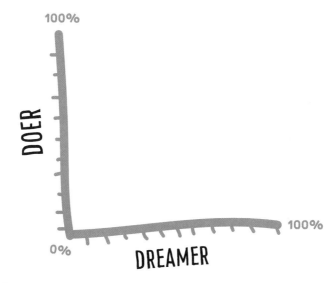

---

* Like in the show, except for the fact that she doesn't live in my apartment or in New York City at all.

EXERCISE

In the above graph, draw a black dot to mark where you stand right now in terms of dreaming and doing. Then draw a star where you want to be a few months from today. Add today's date on top of your dot and a desired date on top of your star to give yourself a deadline.

Doers *do* have fears, don't get me wrong. They *are* sometimes afraid to try* and are not necessarily fearless. They are just *more* afraid of not even trying at all than of failing.

Speaking of failing, in 2017 I did something that was very upsetting to my superego** but that turned me into the ultimate doer.

2017 NEW YEAR'S RESOLUTION

At the beginning of this chapter I told you about my idea to turn my fear into my goal. And to get there, I only had ONE New Year's resolution: to become immune to failure. And just like that, *starting things* became my thing.

During that year I:

● Launched a new YouTube series and podcast called *Dear Younger Self* to empower teenagers to change their perspective on fear and follow their gut.

---

* Read Veronica's answers at the end of this chapter in relation to the fear of failing!

** Remember I said the superego likes the status quo and avoids failure at all times? #SorryNotSorry

- Committed to another 100-day project, this time, an illustrated one via Instagram. I called it "Courage Is," and the idea was to illustrate 100 different definitions of courage—I'm definitely NOT an illustrator, btw!
- Became a nomad halfway through the year. We put everything we own in a tiny storage unit and traveled from one place to the other.
- Launched a clothing line for Hello Fears with some of my most memorable lines. From T-shirts and stickers to hats and chokers, we had it all.
- Hired our first official employees!

That is a just a sample of the things I started in 2017, and I have to say that I became dangerously immune to the fear of failure.

That year I learned a ton! Did I fail? You bet I did. I failed at running a successful business.

As it turns out, I became pretty good at starting things and not so good at finishing them. However, if my New Year's resolution was to fail, goal achieved, right?

- I didn't finish my 100-day illustration project. I got to #86. Close.
- I abandoned that podcast after fourteen episodes.
- I stopped creating videos for YouTube once the nomad life took off.
- I ended up with so much merchandise on my hands that I gave it away to people in need in Venezuela.

- I had to fire my first employees because I had no idea what to ask from them.

You could say that I failed, but I would argue that I also learned lessons I could never have learned if I hadn't tried, like:

- The importance of setting measurable goals for myself and my team.
- That having a strategy is more important than having the perfect product.
- The meaning behind the popular saying, "hire slow, fire fast."
- That compulsive multitasking is not the right way to run a business.
- That a new lifestyle requires new sacrifices. We can't have it all. No matter how much we try.
- To say no after saying yes to every single idea that crossed my mind.
- The value in finishing a project before starting the next one.

This is the first time that I am admitting those failures and lessons publicly. So, if you've been following me on social media for a while, you're probably wondering why you had no idea about these flops, right? And the reason is because on social media, everybody looks like they're doing GREAT!

EVERYBODY IS DOING GREAT

Have you noticed that Instagram is the weapon we use to hurt our ego the most? We may not rationalize it that way before opening the app. We may say things like, "Let me clear my mind and see what other people are up to for a second," or, "Let me find some inspiration; screw Pinterest, let me browse through Instagram and see what I find!"

No one says, "Let me ruin my day by seeing how everybody else is constantly winning at life, being successful, independent, and happy, going to the most amazing places, and eating at the most amazing restaurants while I'm here at work eating last night's chicken in front of my computer."

The problem with Instagram, and any other social media really, is that we only get to see like 2 percent of that person's life. Unsurprisingly, it's the 2 percent that is going amazingly well, or that they pretend is. And immediately we all assume that that person's life must be *perfect,* they never get rejected, and they never make a mistake! It happens to all of us, and it really messes with our minds.

Suddenly our superego gets bigger. Now, it's not enough to have a good job and provide for your family; you also need to have a side hustle, be the perfect mom or dad, nail some DIY projects, and write deep thoughts on posts daily. Seriously, it's impossible to keep up. But that is what you see other women and men do on Instagram. Instead of feeling inspired by them, you start to feel pressured. The expectations are unrealistic. We see everybody else so happy and accomplished as if it were EASY! The moment it gets a little bit hard, we assume we are failing, and we may even stop trying.

I've been a victim of people sharing only the great 2 percent of their lives, making me feel as if my life is not good enough compared to theirs. I now have one important rule when it comes to sharing my life on social media: #ShareTheWholeStory.

A STORY ABOUT REJECTION

A few months ago, I received two emails from different agencies who were considering me for their clients' campaigns. It is unusual for me to receive these kinds of emails, so inevitably I was dancing all over the place when I read about both campaigns:

The first one was a TV spot for Honda. And the other campaign was for Olay. They were both looking for real, authentic, and brave women who were having an impact on society. The Olay campaign was called "Face Anything," and the idea behind it was to highlight courageous women. That's not all. They wanted me to have my own spread in—wait for it...*Vogue*'s September Issue. If that wasn't enough, there was going to be a poster of my face covering one of Union Square subway station's walls, and also one on one of Times Square's enormous digital billboards. Basically, every girl's dream come true in one campaign for a skincare brand. Say whaaaat?! I couldn't sleep for weeks expecting the good news.

Two weeks later I received an email from Olay's casting agent letting me know that the client "selected other people." Gulp. Hours later, I received an email from Honda's agency saying how sorry they were that their client selected the second option instead of me. I was devastated. Turns out rejection is not our ego's best pal; it hurts as much as failure—even when it's not our fault.

The Four Steps That Helped Me Move Past Rejection

1. **FEEL HURT.** If you got a big NO from someone, either the person you like, the job you wanted, or any opportunity you thought was right for you, it's okay to be sad and heartbroken. This is a necessary stage to experience in order to overcome rejection. If you are like me, your anxiety will turn into a horrible stomachache if you don't process it immediately, and you will be wondering for days, "But, what did I eat?" Your feelings!

It is important that we acknowledge how we feel and take time to heal. Hiding our feelings and toughening up immediately will not allow us to continue with the process and will most likely come back to haunt us later.

2. **STICK TO THE PLAN.** I believe that when things don't happen it's for a reason, and interestingly enough, most of the time, sooner or later, I see what that reason was. Maybe it's a month later that you say, "Wow! Thank God they didn't offer me that job, because if they did then this European relocation would've never happened!" It is that *aha* moment that you were looking for. You've experienced it, right?

It happened to me a month later when the Olay campaign was released. Turns out that the entire campaign was celebrating fearless women, literally using the word *fearless* to describe them. That would've been terrible for my brand, given that I have a huge resistance toward that word and push for the word *brave* instead. *Phew. Thank God I was not part of that campaign!* I thought. I hands down believe that there is a plan for us, and I choose to stick to the plan. At least, that gives me the peace of mind and confidence to move to the next stage of the rejection process:

3. **MOVE ON.** We cannot hold on to the things we didn't get forever. Thinking of all the possible ways we could've done things differently has to have an expiration date. Give yourself a time frame and stick to it. Say something like, "I will continue feeling sorry for myself for the next twelve hours, and then, that's it!" Some people will need a few days; some only need a few minutes. Only you know how much time you need to get over yourself.

According to dialectical behavioral therapy (DBT), the pain of being rejected is inevitable in life, but suffering is optional. This means that when we accept our reality, we are more willing to make the best of our situation and move on; however, when we reject it or fight it, we cause ourselves an unnecessary dose of pain and suffering. Ignore the "why me?" question or the "this is not fair!" comment, and set a deadline for yourself—one you are committed to respecting. After that, this situation must be history.

4. **FLIP IT AROUND.** Feeling hurt after rejection is one thing we can all relate to. So, how can you turn your experience into a relatable story and use it to connect with other people?

When I received both rejection emails, I did something I shouldn't have: I started scrolling through Instagram as a way to clear my mind. Instagram just reminded me that everybody else was getting what they wanted, and I was not. I started feeling envious and even more disappointed—thinking that I was never going to attain the things I wanted.

As I was scrolling down and feeling sorry for myself, I had a moment of realization: It is not that these people are not being rejected—they are! They're simply not sharing their rejection stories on social media. That's it!

I went against my superego request and publicly admitted what I was going through. I told my Instagram audience that I too get rejected. And to show them how, I shared the screenshots I took of both rejection emails.

All of a sudden, I started receiving hundreds of messages from people sharing THEIR stories. I received screenshots of emails from people who were being laid off, people who were getting rejected from the schools they applied to, and even a message from a girl who at that very moment was being dumped by her boyfriend OVER TEXT MESSAGE. And they all thanked me, from the bottom of their hearts, for making them feel good about their lives again.

And that is how the *#ShareTheWholeStory* campaign was born.

Sharing stories of vulnerability makes us realize we are not alone, and we all feel better keeping each other company. So, I challenge you to share your failures and rejection stories with others as often as you share your wins. You will be surprised by how people react to vulnerability, and you will receive a ton of support when you need it the most.

My mission is to maintain some balance: share the good stuff, why not? But also share the not-so-great stuff. You might be surprised to hear that the not-so-great stuff gets me even more engagement, compassion, loyalty, support, empathy, and empowerment from those who read my content. People are so eager to converse about these heavy topics because very few people dare to share the failures, like the rejection letters they get, the mistakes they've made, and the amount of sacrifice behind their success.

I GET FOOLED TOO

When I started writing this book I went from *I hope some people buy this book and find value in it* to *Is it possible that this book can turn into a bestseller overnight and sell millions of copies?* That last—and pretty naïve—thought was a consequence of a post I read on Instagram.

Rachel Hollis recently hit two million copies sold with her book *Girl, Wash Your Face* and posted about it on social media. Her success made me believe I should also achieve those kinds of milestones with my book, this book you're currently reading. But I didn't get the whole story.

Later that night as I was telling Adam all about Rachel Hollis's two million copies sold and the possibility of my book getting close to that, he asked me a simple question: "Did you read the full caption?"

At that point, I realized I hadn't. I read the first few lines of copy:

> Passed 2 MILLION books sold this week! You guys! Look what you did!! … This is UNBELIEVABLE. YOU are unbeliev-able!! Thank you, thank you, thank you!

I actually stopped reading after the second "thank you." That was enough for me to question if my book could be as good as hers and suddenly change my goal from selling a few copies to help people to hitting two million books sold out of the blue.

What I was missing was this *very important* part of that post's caption:

> I am so grateful for this year and this book and even more grateful for the five that came before it. Because this isn't my first release. I know what it is to have a book fail. I know what it feels like to sit at a book signing for hours and not have one person walk up to my table. I know what it's like to want so badly to have just one person care about my work, I will NEVER get over that there are now millions of people who do. I prom-ise you I won't ever take it for granted. #GirlWashYourFace

Chills? Me too.

I love following people like Rachel Hollis because, besides being such doers, they share the whole story and say things as they are, no sugarcoating necessary. And us, the readers, we must not only curate our feed to make sure we are only following the influencers with enough courage to share the whole story, but it is also our responsibility to read the full caption. Because the more we fool ourselves, the bigger our superego gets and the bigger the distance between us and our goals.

In an effort to make the world a superego friendly place—meaning filled with fewer external expectations to be perfect and having everything figured out without setbacks—I have two messages.

To all the content creators reading this book:

Next time you think about sharing a post on Instagram about your happy kids, think about the moms who are having a really tough time and all women who cannot even conceive and will be reading your post. Be mindful of them when writing your copy. When you share how much you love your boo, think about your readers who may be in the middle of an ugly divorce or a breakup. Do express your love if it's genuine, but keep it down to earth and use humor and empathy to share the honesty of a real, human relationship. When you post about your perfect, healthy, fit body, take into account those with terrible self-image problems who may be browsing Instagram to distract themselves from their own insecurities and may just happen to stumble upon your #beachbody post. These thoughts can help us be more mindful when we share our lives online and can even inspire us to add a little realness to it so we sound more grounded and cause less harm. Let's give our readers the idea that they too can make it, despite any failures and hiccups along the way.

To all the browsers out there who love to scroll:

I beg you, do not believe everything you see on Instagram. No one's life is perfect. I love what therapist Whitney Hawkins Goodman wrote in one of her posts: "The parenting expert you see on Instagram; her kids throw tantrums in the grocery store. The couples' therapist fights with their spouse. They might even yell. The dietician gives her kids fast food sometimes when she's tired. The fitness blogger skips the gym and has bad body image days." And I may add: the motivational speaker who talks about overcoming fear is terrified of life sometimes (yup, that's me).

The next time you browse through Instagram, think about all the setbacks that are not in the picture but that may still be present in that person's life. That is a defense mechanism that is totally healthy and acceptable. If people are not sharing the whole story, create the story in your mind and help yourself see the human, imperfect side we all have. Never assume that it was just easy for the other person to accomplish success. Re-create in your mind the sleepless nights, the rejection emails, the times they asked themselves, "Will I make it?" and the countless hours put into the work they've created. *The hustle is real.*

THE HUSTLE IS INVISIBLE

Most people *only* show results because the hustle is not pretty or fun or entertaining. On the contrary, the hustle is slow, tedious, full of baggy eyes, late nights, and empty coffee mugs. Who wants to see that?

The problem is that when we hide the hustle, we take away from our success and make our achievements look effortless.

When others get inspired by your achievements and say something like, "I want to be just like Michelle, travel the world and inspire people with my message," they have no clue about the amount of work that is required. They get easily frustrated as soon as they don't meet their goals the first time around. I dare you to change these perceptions and show off your hustle!

Just like Rachel Hollis didn't sell two million copies the first time around, and I didn't get booked by clients right after releasing my TEDx Talk, you probably won't become an overnight success either. And that is okay for two reasons:

1. There is no such thing as an overnight success. What may look like overnight to you actually took years in the making. You just weren't there while all of that was happening.

2. If it were that easy, everybody would make it. Making it is only for the ones who persevere, those who are able to reframe the concept of failure.

Because what comes easy goes easy, but we want *our* success to stay, grow, overcome obstacles, and prevail over time. Therefore we must understand it won't come easy, but if we open the necessary doors to get there, we'll get there, eventually, and stay there.

And before we move into the next chapter, which is one of my favorites, I want to share with you one of the most memorable stories I've heard related to failure.

"HOW DID YOU FAIL TODAY?"

That's the question her dad used to ask Sara and her brother every night while having dinner. Both of them had to come up with at least one story of failure to tell their dad every night.

Her dad would celebrate and high-five whoever shared a good story of failure over dinner. "Dad, I tried this new thing, and totally failed!" Sara would say. "Good job, sweetheart," her dad would answer. But whenever there were no stories of failure of rejection, her dad would be totally crushed and disappointed.

Sara and her brother were aware of the importance of trying new things and failing as a way to grow, learn, and develop thick skin.

Opening doors and facing the unknown became a healthy habit for these siblings.

Today, Sara Blakely is the founder of Spanx—and one of the most influential and wealthiest women alive. And while she may have a lot of fears, failing will not be the one stopping her.

So, I ask you: How did you fail today? I challenge you to hold this question in your mind throughout the day and return to this chapter later to answer it.

Today I failed at:

FROM DREAMER TO DOER

Interview with Verónica Ruiz del Vizo

Verónica Ruiz del Vizo is a self-made entrepreneur. She founded her own digital advertising agency, Mashup, when she was eighteen years old and immediately started working with big clients such as PepsiCo, MasterCard, Doritos, and Smirnoff. Now in her early thirties, she has grown her company to more than one hundred employees and works with brands all over the world. Recently, she created an online educational platform, DAR Learning, aimed at empowering Hispanic women to develop their full potential.

MICHELLE: How do you perceive failure?

VERONICA: I fail the moment that I (1) stop listening to my intuition, (2) stop betting on my own talent, (3) allow self-doubt to take over, and (4) drift apart from my values.

MICHELLE: What is one lesson you learned by failing?

VERONICA: Failure has been my greatest teacher in life. It has taught me that the fear in our heads can be loud, even louder than our intuition sometimes. It is our job to lower the volume of fear and crank up our intuition's volume, because only then will we be able to act according to our values and our priorities. I also learned to be a more forgiving and kinder leader to people around me. Because as much as we want to, we can't keep everything under control at all times, so we have to trust ourselves and our teams more. Mistakes will happen, and that is okay!

VERONICA: The only way to obtain exceptional results is by taking exceptional risks. We understand as a company that it is through innovation that we can achieve the unimaginable and become pioneers in our field. Choosing to stay in the comfort zone may keep us safe for awhile, but it will also keep us from making an impact.

MICHELLE: What is your company's culture around risk-taking?

MICHELLE:
What has been your proudest accomplishment?

VERONICA:
I'm proud of my seventeen-year-old self. I lost my mom that year, and so I decided to believe in myself, be my biggest ally, and double down on my projects. That not only saved me from an emotional breakdown, but it also led me to where I am today. Now, my biggest challenge is to continue being my resilient and confident self, even when the waters seem calmer.

SIX Key TAKEAWAYS

Go to hellofearsbook.com to explore more activities that will make this chapter jump off the page.

→ Watch a Gary Vee talk about going after and grabbing what we want.

→ Learn more about Verónica Ruiz del Vizo by watching a short interview we did together and following her on Instagram @veroruizdelvizo.

→ Check out the *Dear Younger Self* YouTube series.

→ Explore Olay's Face Anything campaign and the brave women they chose instead of me.

→ Listen to the Sara Blakely episode on *How I Built This*.

→ Rent the movie *Jobs* and get inspired to change the world.

→ Read Rachel Hollis's book, *Girl, Wash Your Face*—come on, let's help her reach ten million copies sold!

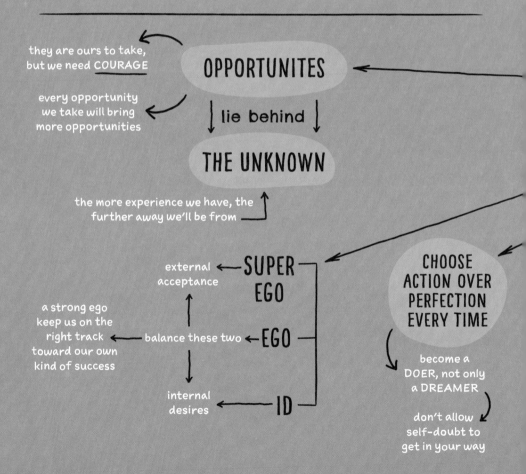

they are ours to take, but we need COURAGE

OPPORTUNITES

every opportunity we take will bring more opportunities

↓ lie behind ↓

THE UNKNOWN

the more experience we have, the further away we'll be from

external acceptance ← **SUPER EGO**

a strong ego keep us on the right track toward our own kind of success ← balance these two ← **EGO**

internal desires ← **ID**

CHOOSE ACTION OVER PERFECTION EVERY TIME

become a DOER, not only a DREAMER

don't allow self-doubt to get in your way

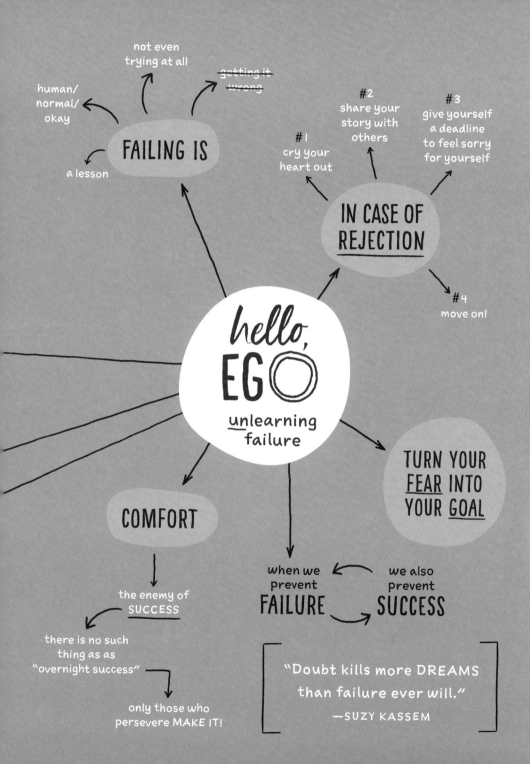

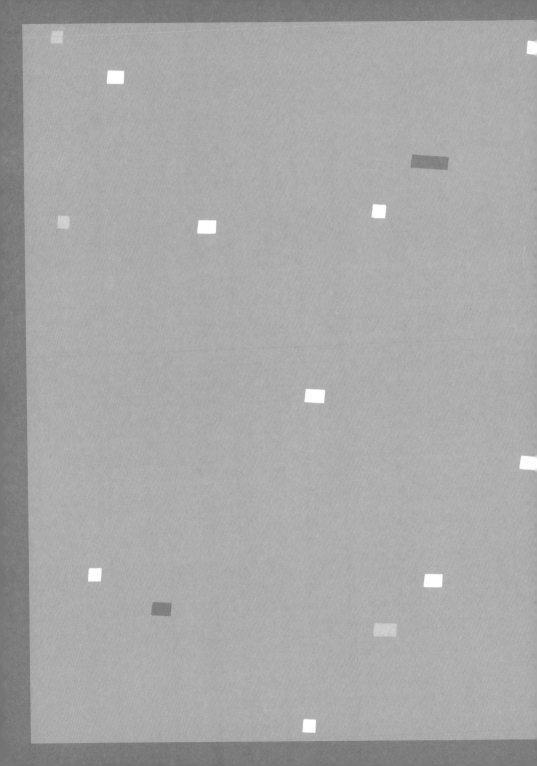

SEVEN

hello,
GROWTH

OVERCOMING THE
WTF AM I DOING? STAGE

"I'm quitting my job."

THAT'S THE TEXT MESSAGE I received on June 14, 2016, at 3:45 p.m. from Adam as he sat in his boss's office. The message came with a picture of his boss, who was cluelessly minding his own business only a few feet away from Adam.

"You what?! Wait a minute. Let's discuss that tonight over dinner. Do NOT quit your job!" And that was my answer.

Earlier that day Adam had a conversation with a person, also called Michele, but with one L, who works at a prestigious management company that represents speakers such as Brené Brown and Shawn Achor. During that first conversation, Michele with one L told Adam about the enormous potential for Michelle (me, two Ls) in the industry. Michele is one of those people who love what they do so much that they go above and beyond to help others who cross their paths—lucky us!

Michele spent an hour on the phone with Adam teaching him all about the speaking industry and helping him position me as the up-and-coming next big thing.

That fifty-two-minute phone call was the catalyst for Adam wanting to jump ship, say bye-bye to his stable job, and join me full-time in launching my speaking career.

Welcome to the most crucial chapter of this book.

If you are also in the middle of making an important life decision and you find yourself trying to choose between two things, and the option you want the most is the scariest one, forget about the rest of the chapters. THIS is the one you must read, until the very end. Welcome to Chapter 7, where we talk about the six-stage process of facing our fears and how to get over the ONE stage that keeps most of us from taking action. I call it the WTF Am I Doing? stage.

PROS AND CONS

That night, Adam came home at around 7:00 p.m. with a huge pad of Post-it Notes. HUGE. Have you seen those? They look like Post-it Notes for giants—they're actually called Easel Pads, in case you want to get them. He also brought a couple of markers so we could create a list of all the pros and cons of saying goodbye to our only reliable and steady source of income to start a movement and become full-time entrepreneurs. So, after a lovely ten-minute dinner of takeout sushi, we put two of the sticky giant Post-it Notes on our wall. One was for pros and the other was for cons, and we started writing away everything we could think of. As I anticipated, two sheets were not enough. We spent the next hour debating and scribbling stuff on paper. We were going nuts! This had to be one of the toughest and most exciting decisions we've ever made.

I had already left my job almost a year prior to that moment. So, as you can imagine, after living for eleven months on only one salary in NYC, we had depleted our hard-earned savings. We were definitely not comfortable making the decision to go all-out with entrepreneurship, but our experience showed us that there was a viable business here and that with all of our efforts combined we had a good chance of making it work.

These were the main points that helped us make a decision:

Cons of Adam quitting his job:

1. No stability whatsoever. We only had a couple of (poorly) paid events lined up at that point and savings to survive for the next two months under extreme frugality.

2. No health insurance or any of the other benefits provided by his job.

3. Uncertainty. Lots of it.

Pros of Adam quitting his job:

1. Doubling down efforts to launch our own business together—instead of him having to work from 9:00 a.m.–6:00 p.m. on his job and then from 8:00 p.m.–2:00 a.m. on this business—like we had been doing for the last year.

2. He could travel with me to all of my talks without having to ask for permission or use all of his vacation, holiday, and sick days.

3. We would finally become entrepreneurs, like we've always dreamed of. The sky is the limit, and the stars are in our favor!

We spent all night debating between two choices:

STABILITY, which was a choice based on fear and comfort.

INDEPENDENCE, which was a choice based on growth and progress.

Comfort is the choice that feels safe on the inside. It's what your entire body is begging you to choose, because it requires less work, less fear, less trouble. So, it is really hard to go against what your body is telling you to do and listen to your intuition, the one that is telling you which one is the right choice for you, the growth choice.

Sometimes it is not easy to define which one is the growth choice and which one is the comfort one. It is not necessarily an obvious decision. What may seem like a growth choice (i.e., a new job offer with higher pay at a prestigious corporation) may be your comfort choice (that job may be better than what you have now, but will prevent you from spending more hours working on your side hustle that can eventually turn into your ideal full-time job).

"What is the option that scares us the most?" That's the question I asked Adam at 4:00 a.m. that day. And based on that answer we decided to go to sleep and face the day with our decision...

"You will either step forward into growth, or step back into safety."
—ABRAHAM MASLOW

Life will always give us choices: some will take us back into our comfort zone; others will challenge us, but help us grow. The important thing here is to identify which one is the growth choice and choose that one despite the fear of what it may bring. In fact, that's the best way to tell them apart: **growth is—most of the time—the scariest choice to make.**

Now I want you to think about a decision you have in front of you, one that can lead you to achieve your next goal. It doesn't have to be as big as changing your whole career—it could even be a small decision that has the potential to help you become a better version of yourself. For example: Should I: Ask him out? Move away from home? Accept that job offer? Try yoga? Eat healthier? Buy a car?

Should I:

Write down the two main choices you have in regard to that decision:

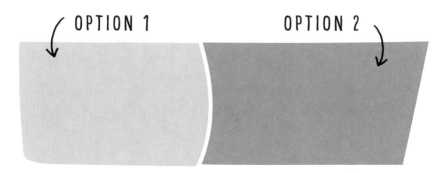

OPTION 1   OPTION 2

Now circle the one option that scares you the most. Keep that in mind as we move forward with this chapter.

FEAR-FACING PROCESS

There is a six-stage process to facing a fear—ANY fear. This is not something I read online; this is something I figured out on my own in the course of facing 100 fears myself. I realized that it doesn't matter how many fears you face—we all go through the same process over and over again.

The Discovery Stage

Imagine you are living your life, going about your routine and having a normal Tuesday afternoon. You may be at work, school, home, a bar, or wherever you find yourself during a not-so-special Tuesday afternoon. Suddenly, as you are scrolling down your social media feed you see something that makes you think, "Wow, I would never do that," or one of those expressions that may lead you to consider something you've never considered doing before. It could be a post of someone saying, "Moving to India for a year!" or "Getting ready to perform at an open mic tonight!" or "Buying our first home!" or, "Going back to school after three kids!"—whatever scares the crap out of you. Maybe it's a text message you get, with an unexpected invitation someone sends your way, like, "Hey, Michelle, what about volunteering abroad together this year?" That split moment of realization that something you haven't considered suddenly makes you open your eyes real big and say "wait, what?"—THAT is the discovery stage.

The Denial Stage

Immediately after discovering that you are scared of doing something you'd never even considered a few minutes ago, your mind comes up with two hundred completely "valid" reasons why you shouldn't face that fear. "I'm not in shape to do that," or "My parents would go crazy if I do that," or "I would not be able to afford that." Anything we have to tell ourselves so we can sleep well at night, go back to our comfort zone, and forget we even considered taking our chances. That is the denial stage, and sadly, most people stay there, surrounded by excuses they validate to stay comfy.

The Determination Stage

The few people who make it past the denial stage realize that their "valid" reasons are just excuses and mainly their fear talking. They think to themselves: *What if I do it and things go right?* Suddenly, expectations and excitement kick in, and without thinking too much about it, you're already making plans to face your fear and win! That is the determination stage. You are 100 percent determined to making it happen. Look at you, you're so pumped!

But, between the determination stage and the action stage, there is a stage that it is very hard to avoid, one that keeps most of us from taking action. I call it:

The WTF Am I Doing? Stage

This is the moment you ask yourself in a deep, slow voice, "What did I get myself into?" You are moments away from taking action, but your fear has started to kick in. You are now considering all the worst-case scenarios, and your mind is convincing you that you most likely will... die. You may die out of embarrassment, emotional pain, or real physical pain—I mean, that parachute may not be working after all. What if taking action only leads to failure? Yep, that is most likely what will happen. Or at least, that is what you are convincing yourself. Only the very, *very* brave people are able to get over their worst thoughts and move past this stage, and that's what THIS chapter is for, to help you **take action.**

The Action Stage

"You Are Here" the map would read. This map is similar to the one you would find inside a mall but much simpler. This map has a huge circle with the words *Comfort Zone* written in the middle and a small star far outside that circle with the words *You Are Here*. That is what happens when we land in the action stage. Here's when we get

**YOU ARE
HERE**

COMFORT
ZONE

hella uncomfortable, and we take action. Here's when we say: "Thanks for everything, but I quit!" or "Hey, Dad, I'm gay!" or "3, 2, 1, jump!" or "I do" or "One-way ticket to Thailand, please. Yep, just one!" or "I want a divorce, and I'm keeping the cactus!"

The Celebration Stage

Have you ever felt proud of yourself? Like very proud? Like doing a happy dance kind of proud? I know for a fact that I never felt that kind of proud of myself before in my life. I mean, I graduated from college with a 4.0 GPA, I got married to an amazing man, I did all the things I was expected to do and feel pride in. For me, those things weren't outside of my comfort zone. So, accomplishing them didn't make me feel particularly *proud* of myself. I thought: Check! One less thing I need to worry about. But, proud? Nah. Proud, *real* proud, is what you feel when you want something so bad that you're willing to fight the WTF Am I Doing? stage and take action. That makes you feel really proud—regardless of the outcome. Stop for a moment to celebrate and give yourself a pat on the back before you move on with your life and worry about what comes next.

Now I challenge you to, in this moment, consider facing a fear, even if it's a small one, and experience the process I just described. Are you in the denial stage already? Come on!

Most people ask me about my *secrets* to getting over the WTF Am I Doing? stage and facing my fears. But, to be honest, there are no secrets here, just one simple question that flips everything around. One question that gives me the superpower of having x-ray vision. One question that changed my life, and now, the lives of many.

GETTING OVER THE WTF AM I DOING? STAGE

On October 18, 2015, I faced my one hundredth fear. In the next chapter of this book I will tell you how I got to speak at TEDxHouston, one of my ultimate dreams—and also one of my ultimate fears. But, for now I will share with you what happened on that day that allowed me to face my fear and take action.

It was 2:15 p.m., and I was shaking. I was about to go on stage when I started feeling sick to my stomach.

Why did I not consider this moment when I decided to speak at TEDxHouston? I was in such internal struggle at that point that my WTF Am I Doing? stage was out of control! The truth is that I was about to go on stage to motivate people to face their fears and at that moment I had no idea how to control mine... I felt a bit impostor-like, as though I were a dietitian telling you to eat healthy while eating cookies in front of you. What I needed more than anything was a magic wand or an actual tool that could help me face my fear of going on stage. Sadly, I didn't have one.

My walk from the green room to the stage was painful, to say the least. I was more terrified than I've ever been in my entire life. I had a lot at stake. I mean, it was my 100th fear. I not only had my parents watching, I had my professors from the School of Visual Arts watching, and a few thousand people who were following this project. Plus, the talk was livestreamed, so all of those people were going to be watching *live*.

I was not walking alone to the stage. One of the TEDx volunteers was walking along with me. Her only job that day was to mic me up and lead me to the stage. But, as we were walking along, she looked at me, even smiled at me, but the look I returned was not what she was expecting. My face revealed how scared I was to go onstage. When she realized I was about to start walking the other way, back to my green room, back to my hotel room, back to my plane, back to NYC, back to Fear #99, she grabbed me by the shoulders, looked me in the eyes, and said: "Michelle! Sweetie, you've got this. It will be all right. Plus, what's the worst that could happen?"

Have you ever asked yourself, or someone else, this question before? Such an innocent and well-intended question, right? Sure. It didn't take long before thousands for negative thoughts attacked my brain, thoughts that weren't even there in the first place.

What's the worst that could happen? Well...

- I could forget my speech.
- I could freeze.
- I could embarrass myself.
- I could disappoint my family, my professors, and thousands of followers.
- Or, I could just totally fail.

THAT is the worst that could happen. Thank you for asking! I feel much better now! Where's the mic? Oh, it's on me! Not anymore, byyyyyeeeee!

As I was coming up with all the possible worst-case scenarios in my head, trying to answer the volunteer's question, it hit me: *How am I supposed to gather the courage that I need if I'm only considering the negative outcomes?* It was only then that I decided to flip the question around, and I humbly asked myself, "Michelle...**what's the BEST that can happen?**"

All of a sudden, I was able to see the possibilities that were hiding behind my fears, the REAL reasons why I decided to do a TEDx Talk in the first place. So, I thought of some of the best-case scenarios:

- What if I do a good job?
- What if I remember ALL of my speech?
- What if I make people laugh, engage, or even get emotional?
- What if I make my family proud, my professors proud, and my community proud?
- What if I make MYSELF proud?
- What if I actually inspire people in the audience to take action?

Unexpectedly, I started to feel **less fear** and **more excitement**. Right on time! Because in that precise moment of peace, I heard the presenter say *"Give it up for...Michelle Poler!"*

Without knowing it, I was triggering my Behavioral Activation System, which led me to overcome the WTF Am I Doing? stage and take action.

RISKS VS. REWARDS

Let's get geeky for a moment here: as humans, we are born with a reptilian brain as part of our nervous system. That is where our fear lives. Since we were born with that part of the brain already installed, we are wired to think about risk automatically at ALL times, mostly right before taking action—hence, the WTF Am I Doing? stage. But in order to face our fears, and make a habit out of that, we must rewire our brain to focus on the reward instead of on the risk.

According to psychologist Jeffrey Grey there are two primary systems influencing every decision that we make: the Behavioral Activation System (BAS) and the Behavioral Inhibition System (BIS).

The way I see it, the **Behavioral Inhibition System** responds to risk and stops us from taking action. It is the system that begs us to stay in our comfort zone and maintain the status quo. It is the system that chooses only to focus on the risks involved and asks us to act accordingly.

For example, as you already know, at the beginning of my talks, right after the presenter announces my name, I come on stage dancing reggaetón, and I go ALL OUT! And if that isn't shocking and uncomfortable enough for the audience, I ask people to dance with me. The majority of the audience members normally choose to stay petrified in their seats and ignore the fact that music is playing and that someone (me) is clearly asking them to stand up and dance. All of them are reacting to the Behavioral Inhibition System. They quickly consider all the possible risks and make the choice to stay comfortable in their seats waiting for someone else to be on the spot.

The few brave people who decide to accept the challenge and start shaking their booties are the ones who intentionally paid attention to what their **Behavioral Activation System** was telling them. This system is triggered by reward, and encourages us to take action. So, in that split second, they thought of possible rewards like waking themselves up, showing off their moves, or doing something that may be completely outside of their comfort zone, but that will make them feel proud of themselves later.

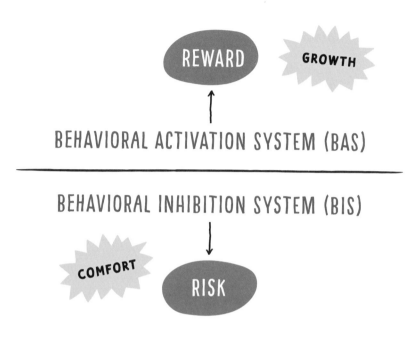

In order to choose growth over comfort, the first thing we need to do is focus on the rewards. Ask yourself the question: "What's the BEST that can happen?" and write down a list of all the possible best-case scenarios. Then, it's just a matter of focusing on those things to take action. That is the best way to rewire our brains and get into the habit of taking more risks. And the more you do it, the more naturally this way of thinking will come to you.

I don't need a magic wand anymore; I have my own superpower, and now you do too.

X-RAY VISION

The reason why I call this tool my superpower is because I feel as if I have X-ray vision when I take advantage of it.

When we are entering the WTF Am I Doing? stage, we tend to forget our WHY—our main reasons why we decided to face a certain fear in the first place—and all we see is a brick wall in front of us. Every brick has some negative message like, "you won't be able to do this," or, "you are not good enough for this," or "who do you think you are?" That is just our fear talking. The only way to see through those fears, those heavy orange bricks, is by asking ourselves the question: WTBTCH (what's the best that can happen?). That is the best chance we have to see through the fear and focus on the reward. That is what will give us a better chance to trigger our BAS (Behavioral Activation System).

Which system do you respond to most of the time? Do you make most of your decisions based on the risk or on the rewards that a certain opportunity may bring you?

circle one

- The Behavioral Activation System (BAS)—I respond to the rewards more often
- The Behavioral Inhibition System (BIS)—I respond to the risks more often

Before we move on to the next section, I want you to ask yourself, "What's the BEST that can happen?" if you chose to go for the option you circled a few pages ago. Write down five possible rewards that taking action could bring you:

If I,

this could happen:

CONTAGIOUS

Growth is personal; what may be growth for me may be comfort for you and vice versa. And what is growth for you today could turn into comfort in a few months or years from now. Only you can determine what growth means for you in this moment.

What's magical is that regardless of what growth means for you, when you decide to share that story with others, that simple act of choosing courage can inspire many to do the same. Fear is one of the most relatable feelings in the world; that's why it has so much power. You can infect someone with fear, or you can dose them with courage. I choose to spread courage, and these are a few of my favorite stories of people who have heard my message and taken action. Maybe you can relate to some of them as well.

Seven Stories of Growth from Everyday People

1.

"Growth for me was to speak up despite my stutter."
By Sajia L.

Right after my parents separated, my stuttering began. It's like my throat gets stuck, which causes me to repeat letters (especially the vowels) when I'm speaking. There is nothing worse than wanting to communicate my thoughts and opinions but not being able to do so because of a situation that goes beyond my control.

When I started working in banking, my stuttering became more evident, especially when I had to talk to my boss. Due to his hasty style, there have been several occasions in which he, literally, left me with the words in my mouth—no pun intended.

One day, I gathered the courage I needed, and I said, "I need to tell you something, and I need you to listen to me, because I know that when I stutter you don't listen to me." My boss was paralyzed. Now HE was the one who was speechless. He immediately apologized, and for the first time, he listened.

That moment was a revelation because it showed me that my voice is valuable. Today I recognize and value the action of listening to others more than anything. Listening is the only way to discover the great things that others have to offer us.

2.

"Growth for me was about getting a self-love tattoo, without others' validation."

By Andrea R.

My heart was broken last year, and this is the first time I [had] experienced a heartbreak. The pain was so deep that I really thought I was going to die at some point.

During that time the only thing that could calm my anxiety was the sound of the sea. I downloaded every single meditation app and spent hours looking at the sea not too far from my house. I was mesmerized by the way it moved to and away from me. That's when it hit me: I needed to get a wave tattoo as a way to get over my first heartbreak.

My parents are the most caring people I know, but they don't understand or support modern views on equality, LGBT rights, and a bunch of other stuff—like tattoos. But, despite their disagreement, I still did it. I got a wave tattoo.

It was just a tattoo. But for me it was more than that. It was me standing up for myself, it was me making decisions without my parents' approval, it was me getting out of my first heartbreak, it was me being okay without all the answers, it was me growing, it was me being brave, it was me trusting in myself, it was me full of certainty. It was me flowing.

I realized that I'm not who others want me to be, and that gives me permission to choose who I want to become.

3.

"Growth for me was about traveling solo as a young woman in Latin America."

By Jessica L.

I think it all started with a sticker I received at one of Michelle Poler's presentations.

"If I had the courage, I would..."

I ended up writing, "If I had the courage, I would travel by myself."

Maybe that sticker meant nothing. I didn't have to actually go face that fear, but a few days after that presentation, a friend started chasing her sticker dream! That was the last push I needed to make the decision to travel to Cusco, Peru.

This is the moment when you constantly think of what could go wrong. On the plane, I wrote a note with all my fears as an experiment to see how different the feelings could turn out to be before and after. Surprisingly, everything I doubted or feared then had no relation to the way things actually went. In fact, meeting other solo travelers was like having a small taste of the marvelous things the world has to offer.

I learned about the amazingness of wandering, not wondering how it will go, but sharing in the awe of other people you could meet and the places you could discover. All by being open to the opportunity.

4.

"Growth for me was about returning the ring to my fiancé, weeks before the wedding."

By Laura E.

When my boyfriend proposed to me, I accepted! My future looked pretty amazing at that point. A couple of months went by, and I started experiencing this cold feeling on my chest... It felt as if a huge piece of ice was forcefully melting over my heart.

Over time, the feeling evolved from a melting ice on my chest to a thousand rocks crushing me and barely allowing me to breathe. So, I went to see a therapist. That was the best decision I could've ever made. I was able to see the whole picture from her tiny office.

Even though my fiancé was beyond perfect in the eyes of many, he wasn't perfect for me. I made myself think he was *the one* because of his many admirable and unique qualities. But I was not necessarily in love with him.

On a Wednesday afternoon, I ended the relationship. I realized that no one, except me, is responsible for my happiness, and no one, except me, is capable of fighting for it. I went from thinking I had a big part of my life figured out to suddenly being back to square one. I am 100 percent sure it is for the best.

Life and marriage are hard enough with the *right* person by your side; there's no point in making it more complicated by marrying the wrong person. I finally feel peace in my heart and a new sense of self-love I am enjoying profoundly.

5.

"Growth for me was about feeling proud of being a stay-at-home mom."
By Daniela G.

I always felt I was a free-spirited woman: self-employed, an active traveler, and financially independent. That was my life until I became a mom.

When I got pregnant, the idea of leaving my daughter during the day with a complete stranger while we went to work was just not an option. So I did what I thought wouldn't be so hard to do: take care of my daughter. Full time. Like, 24/7.

Being a full-time mom made me feel like I was small, smaller than the rest. For a long time I felt as if I wasn't enough. I felt ashamed, as if my every day was meaningless to others. This is a consequence of the way society was built, and the pressure we feel to be "someone" in this world.

So, I found some allies: new friends, books, articles, even social media accounts that would help me understand how important this job is. Neuroscience even suggests being close to the mother is fundamental to developing healthy neural connections in the brain.

I've never missed a tooth popping out, my daughter's constant smile, or her first steps. Facing my fear of becoming a stay-at-home-mom not only changed my life, it changed the way I see and understand the world.

6.

"Growth for me was about volunteering abroad to help kids in need."
By Mijal E.

I have always loved to help others, and my dream was to volunteer in an orphanage in Africa. I never did much besides browsing online through pictures and imagining the experience. I guess I was scared of actually going.

Right after my college graduation, one of my really good friends told me she wanted to do it too. We packed our bags and traveled to Kenya for five weeks.

We had no clue of what we got ourselves into. Everything that we once took for granted in our day-to-day lives is a luxury over there. I didn't know I was privileged to have clean water until I lived without it. We didn't have any electricity unless it was a sunny day. Our bathroom was a hole in the ground.

In just a few days, all of my personal fears disappeared, and my only concern was to make those kids happy.

I learned to appreciate the simple things in life. Once you see how happy these kids actually are, you kind of feel guilty about complaining about a rainy day at home.

7.

"Growth for me was to leave my stable job in finance to support my wife's career despite society's expectations."
By Adam Stramwasser

Ever since we got married, my wife, Michelle, and I have helped each other with our projects. We always saw our relationship as a partnership and whatever was best for one was also best for the team.

Right after Michelle's TEDx Talk, we realized there was a huge opportunity. I knew that if I had the time to double down on Michelle's speaking career, we could turn that into our main business. But the thought of renouncing my own career after years of studying and two degrees, forfeiting being the main provider, and being perceived as the husband who works for his wife, shook me. Society's expectations made it all much harder:

"Adam is Michelle's helper."

"Adam just carries Michelle's bags."

"Adam is 'living the life' now that his wife is the provider."

I'm glad I had the courage to listen to my inner voice and not everybody else's. Joining Michelle full-time not only turned us into successful entrepreneurs, but it also led me to discover my passion and build my own personal brand. Otherwise, today I would still be answering to a boss, earning a fraction of what I make, and at a loss trying to find my purpose in life. And Michelle's career never would've taken off in the way it did.

GROWTH

Growth is taking control of our own happiness and our own destiny.

Growth is to be intentional when designing our life.

Growth is doing everything in our power to achieve our goals.

Growth is ignoring others' opinions and following our hearts.

Growth is being the (s)hero of our own life, not the victim.

Growth is freedom.

Growth is a choice.

Before moving on to the next chapter, sign this contract with yourself:

"I, _____, commit to choosing growth over comfort every chance that I get. Because I believe in myself, I deserve to be happy, and my future is in MY hands."

_____

(Your signature here)

SEVEN Key TAKEAWAYS

Go to hellofearsbook.com to explore more activities that will make this chapter jump off the page.

→ Watch my TEDx Talk and the BTS (behind the scenes).

→ Watch Seth Godin's 99U presentation about lizard brain.

→ Read more stories of courage at hellofears.com.

→ Visit @stramhacks on Instagram, Adam's personal brand he discovered after quitting his job.

> "You will either step forward into growth, or step back into safety."
> —ABRAHAM MASLOW

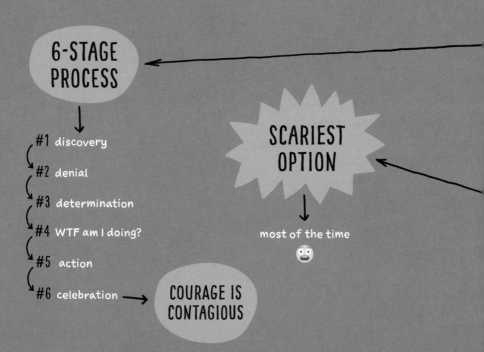

6-STAGE PROCESS

#1 discovery
#2 denial
#3 determination
#4 WTF am I doing?
#5 action
#6 celebration → **COURAGE IS CONTAGIOUS**

SCARIEST OPTION

most of the time
😳

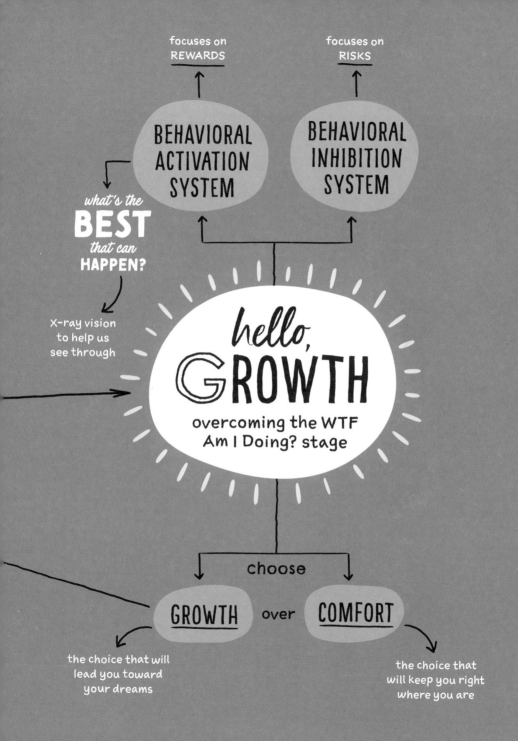

hell-(n)o, HECK YES!

LEARNING HOW TO ASK FOR THE THINGS YOU WANT, NEED, AND DESERVE

Dear Javier, my name is Michelle Poler and I'm currently in the middle of a personal project called "100 Days Without Fear." I already faced 89 fears, and I'm now starting to plan for #100. As this project has gone viral and has taught me more lessons than I could ever imagine, I thought about sharing those valuable learnings with the world through the TEDx platform. Would you be interested in having me present at your event on October 18?

THAT'S THE PRIVATE LINKEDIN MESSAGE I wrote to the TEDxHouston organizer in 2015. He was so excited to hear my story but had one question: Did I have any ties to Houston?

After drafting fifteen different emails with creative ways in which I have ties to Houston, I told him the truth: sadly, no.

The real reason why I chose this specific TEDx was because it was the one scheduled closest in date to the end of my project.

> Dear Michelle, I'm sorry to hear that. We are trying to bring speakers that are relevant to our Houstonian audience and that are preferably local. Good luck with your 100th fear though!

What the heck?!

What would YOU have said to that? I had two options: (1) find a different way to face my 100th fear, or (2) fight for the one challenge I've been dreaming of tackling since I started the project: giving a TEDx Talk. I went with the latter.

All of a sudden, I became the most assertive person I've ever known and sent Javier a long-format email stating *all* the reasons why he should bring me as a speaker for his event, all of which I FIRMLY believed. I talked about how universal the message of bravery can be, so people from Houston, China, Poland, Brazil, and every corner of the world could relate to it. Finally, I promised him that every single person in that audience was going to do an act of courage after watching me present, even if it's a small one. I knew, in my heart, that this talk was going to have a lot of impact on my life and on the lives of many. So, I wrote my heart out and sent him the email without looking back. **I literally had nothing to lose and everything to win.**

It took him ten days to get back to me. TEN long days, full of self-doubt and uncertainty. But after ten days, out of the blue, I received an email from Javier:

> Michelle, I can see that this project has turned you into a resilient person. I admire that. Welcome to TEDxHouston!

Heck yeah!

I experienced *happy tears* for the first time in my life. I read Javier's email and started sobbing, uncontrollably, by myself, sitting in front of my laptop at home. Because (1) I made it to TEDx! My all-time dream. And (2) I freaking earned it. I was shocked that my email worked. That my resilience paid off! When you have the courage to ask for the things you want, you can actually get them. **When you believe in yourself so much, you make others believe in you as well.** That email represented all of that to me and more.

If you are afraid to ask for the things you want, need, and deserve, this chapter is for you. I went from, "The food is good, thanks" when I actually hated it and even found three questionably short curly black hairs in it, to, "Dear waiter, not only did I not like this dish very much, but... look!" And let me say this, I don't consider myself a people pleaser but I avoid confrontation at all costs, so standing up for myself was never in my plans, and *that* was costing me my happiness. My goal with this chapter is to help you become the most assertive person you know.

"NO THANKS"

Do you know what's harder than getting rejected? Rejecting someone or something. Have you ever tried it? I honestly *hate* it. But, throughout this process, I learned the importance of saying no and rejecting the things that we believe are not right for us. Maybe it's a partner who is holding us back, a title that doesn't represent us, a company that doesn't align with our values, a request that makes us uncomfortable, or, in my case, a partnership with a global brand. Here's why:

Let's rewind for a second. After going viral with the 100-day project, a lot of opportunities arose. In the beginning, I was so excited about this phenomenon and all of the attention that I was getting, that I was accepting every podcast invitation, every phone call with potential clients, every media interview or collaboration opportunity. Some of these things were scams, some were a waste of time, but some were pretty legit.

Speaking about legit, one of the emails I received was from an advertising agency I dreamed of working for during my college years. One of their brands was 5 Gum, and their campaign at the time was

"Life Happens in 5," about the five seconds before facing a fear. Such a great fit for my project, right? They contacted me with the hopes of working together and even sponsoring my 100th fear.

At this point, I was facing my 60th fear, so my last fear was pretty far in the future. TEDx was not even an option back then. Having a prestigious ad agency working to come up with a creative way to face my 100th fear sounded pretty darn awesome. I said yes to them and we started working together immediately.

I had an entire creative team working for me, pitching me ideas of things I could do for my last challenge. To me, this was all very hectic and unbelievable. I went from working in an ad agency as part of the creative team, building decks for brands and influencers, to suddenly being the influencer and having brands pitching ME decks. *Huh?*

After weeks of back-and-forth and the 100th fear fast approaching, the team had a *great* idea. Their idea was...A SURPRISE! Yes, they wanted to keep my 100th challenge a surprise, so that I would go to some random place and face a fear that THEY decided I should face. Sure. Looks like they took the fear factor pretty seriously. If the idea was to terrify me, they certainly did—and way ahead of time.

At that point, Adam calls the agency and tells them that they need to run the idea by him first. He knows the project well enough, and ME well enough, to tell if this would be "thanks, but no thanks!"

This is what they had in mind:

OPTION 1: Rappel my way down from one of New York's tallest and most popular buildings, Rockefeller Center.

OPTION 2: Tie me up to the top of a small plane and fly me around Vegas doing all sorts of crazy pirouettes.

Which one would you have chosen? If you are like me, I hope you answered NEITHER to that question in ALL CAPS. The ideas were extreme and not very well aligned with my personal brand and the project. So naturally, Adam discussed the ideas with me first, knowing that I would not agree to do any of those challenges as my most-expected fear.

"Should we let this opportunity go?" I asked Adam. We had so much to lose. Have you ever felt like this? Like you have an amazing opportunity in front of you, but for some reason it doesn't feel right? This deal could've taken my project to a whole new level. And since I had already quit my job weeks ago, the money they were offering could've been very helpful. But deep down something didn't feel right. I knew in my heart that I wanted my last fear to go beyond a physical fear and have a more meaningful impact.

So, after MUCH consideration, I decided to turn down this opportunity and send that first email to Javier about facing my fear at TEDxHouston.

This decision not only marked the beginning of my speaking career, but it showed me the importance of going after the things that feel right in our hearts, and not getting carried away by what *may seem* more glamorous. Turning down 5 Gum felt like facing a fear in itself—the fear of trusting my instincts.

Proving myself right with 5 Gum opened a new world for me, the world of, "No thanks!"

Before doing my project, I used to say "No thanks!" to the things that scare me, no matter the opportunity they represented. Now I say, "No thanks!" to the things that may not add as much value to my life or that don't bring me ultimate happiness.

Because if there is one thing we cannot bring back, it is time. **Time is our most precious asset and the one we most take for granted.**

"LATER"

"SOMEDAY I'LL GO BACK TO SCHOOL AND FINISH MY DEGREE."

"I HATE IT HERE, BUT I WILL QUIT IN THREE YEARS WHEN I REACH A HIGH ENOUGH POSITION."

"EVENTUALLY I'LL BREAK UP WITH HIM/HER."

Sound familiar?

The problem is that our time on earth is limited, and every time we say "yes" to something we don't like, we are saying "no" to what

WHEN YOU BELIEVE IN YOURSELF SO MUCH, YOU MAKE OTHERS BELIEVE IN YOU AS WELL we actually want. It seems as if the fear of CHANGE is greater than the fear of spending our whole lives...waiting.

Saying yes to a boyfriend you are not madly in love with means saying no to the love of your life who is out there, waiting to cross paths with you before it's too late. Saying yes to a job that makes your life miserable is saying no to the perfect job opportunity.

The same goes with the decisions that we make daily. Every time we say yes to hanging out with someone we can't stand, we're saying no to spending more time with the people we care about. Yes to another episode on Netflix is no to making progress on a personal project. Yes to helping someone out means no to helping yourself out.

I'm not asking you to be 100 percent selfish 100 percent of the time, but for some reason, we think it's okay to put ourselves, our needs, and our wants last. It's not okay. **We need to learn to say "No thanks!" more often to others and "Yes please" more often to ourselves, our future, and our happiness.**

> "If you're not saying 'Hell yeah!'
> about something, say no."
> —DEREK SIVERS

A POLITE DECLINE

Saying "no" doesn't have to mean "I don't care about you" or "I don't like you." It just means "I have other priorities right now," or "I need to do this for myself." It's a matter of learning how to politely decline invitations, requests, or favors in a way that we respect our desire without hurting other people.

In my case, I had to decline many requests as a way to make time to write my book, yes, this book. So, emails like "Michelle, can we interview you for a radio station in Berlin?" or even "I live in NYC too, can we meet for coffee someday?" most likely received a polite, but very assertive, no as a reply.

Here are a few steps that can help you decide if you should say yes, and how to say no:

Step #1

Think about a request you received in the last few days, or perhaps one that has been spinning in your head for the last few months. Pay attention to the way you reacted when the question was posted to you in the first place. If you had to use an emoji to describe the face you made as soon as you heard about this request, which emoji would it be?

If your first reaction looked something like the first emoji, and after giving it some thought it still does, what are you still doing reading this book? Go say yes to whoever asked you the question. Go, go, go!

If you selected any of the other emojis, it's most likely a no. But first, read Step #2:

Step #2

Know that you don't have to answer right away. (I'm terrible at this, by the way.) If you were not immediately excited by the request you received, and you are not quite sure how to answer, you can say something like, "What an interesting idea, let me think about it, and I'll get back to you!" And take some time to discuss it with people who you respect and whose opinion you value.

Step #3

Let's say that 50 percent of you wants to say yes, but the other 50 percent is rooting for no. How do you choose? Now is when you have to get REALLY honest with yourself.

Ask yourself the following:

1. Do I want to say yes because of me or because of the other person? (Is someone pushing you to do something you don't feel like doing, but you don't like to disappoint others—mom, partner, boss, friend, brother, daughter...stranger? I've seen it! I've said yes to wine because of a waiter's judgy look!)

2. Do I want to say yes just because I'm afraid to say no? (Do you have an opportunity in front of you that seems like a good one, but deep down in your heart something is telling you to pass, yet you are afraid to miss on that opportunity?)

Making decisions based on other people's needs or making fear-based instead of growth-based decisions will *not* take us very far.

Reasons to say yes:

1. It feels right for you right now—your intuition is telling you to go for it.

2. It could take you where YOU want to go, even though it sounds challenging (careerwise, relationshipwise, healthwise, lifewise...).

3. It brings you joy.

If you end up saying no to this request or opportunity, the way you say no is what matters most:

Step #4

Now that you have defined what you want more of in life, and what you want less of, you can start establishing boundaries. This will help you decline requests so others respect you even more than they already do.

The most important thing about this step is to respect the

boundaries you set for yourself. If you cross your own boundaries, do not think for a minute that someone else will respect them:

- If you say you will only hold meetings on Wednesdays, never schedule meetings on Tuesdays or Fridays.
- If you define that Thursday nights are date night with your partner, make sure to keep those evenings for them.
- If the rule is that people can stay for a maximum of one week at your place, try your best to keep your word, no matter the person or their situation.
- If you decide not to use your phone after 8:00 p.m. to keep you more present with your family at home, don't take calls after that time and ask others not to call you. (Yes, Mom, you too.)

This way we don't sound as if we are making a decision based on the specific person or the request, and they won't be able to take it personally. It should sound more like, "Thank you so much for asking. I appreciate the consideration, but I will have to politely decline since at this time I'm only considering/focusing on/using my free time to/accepting [fill in the blank]." That way it feels more general, you don't need to get into the specifics, it leaves the door open for future opportunities, and it shows that you know how to set boundaries and respect your own time. And there is something very admirable about that.

In fact, **saying no to the people you love deepens the trust.** Yup, just like that.

When you say no in the right way, your loved ones will understand it is because you are honoring yourself. It lets them know that they can also say no to you and that you want them to honor themselves. When the yes comes, they will know you are actually excited to do whatever you said yes to, and they will get the best out of you. And it keeps resentment out of the relationship because you can both be honest about your priorities, wants, and needs.

What NOT to do when rejecting someone or something:

- Blame someone else.
- Define a boundary, and then cross it.
- Make up different excuses for different people.
- Imply with either words or your body language that you might change your mind if they are persistent. (Beware of not sending mixed signals—say NO with your entire body and make eye contact when speaking.)
- Say yes instead of no. Sounds silly, but some of us easily succumb to pressure. We start our sentence with no and along the way we end up saying, "Well, maybe. I guess...yes. Definitely YES." I've done it!

Assertiveness Is the Key

That's all it takes to ask for the things we want and reject the ones we don't.

Being assertive means being able to stand up for your own or other people's rights in a calm and positive way, respecting yourself and others without being aggressive or imposing your views.

FIGHT WITH KINDNESS

I was traveling with Adam, going from one youth leadership event to the other when we had an incident that almost cost us our trip.

After having to deplane our original aircraft due to a malfunction, the airline put us on a much later flight with a different route. Was I excited about this change? Heck no. But the last thing I wanted was to miss our event and disappoint 6,000 high school students.

Right before taking off, the flight attendant approached our emergency exit seats and mumbled a question. "Are you willing and able to assist in case of an emergency?" is the *standard* question flight attendants ask before takeoff to those seated in the emergency exit seats. I was already watching a show on Netflix, so I looked up and answered yes to her question without thinking about it.

Turns out, the flight attendant didn't ask the standard question this time. She asked, "Do you have any questions regarding the emergency exit seats?" And I said yes. Big forking mistake. This lady was in no mood for jokes or misunderstandings. She immediately ordered me to move to the back of the plane. I asked her to PLEASE forgive me and repeat the question. But instead, she repeated, "Stand up now and sit in the back of the plane." *Seriously?*

Out of pure frustration, I took my phone out to record her. Which was inappropriate and a huge mistake, guys. The flight attendant was so mad that, after forcing me to delete the video, she tried to escort us off the plane.

Missing that flight was NOT an option. After a lot of begging on our part, she allowed us to stay on the condition that she would keep our phones for the rest of the flight. Whatever. We sat at the back of the plane, full of shame, and shaky with nerves!

Midair, Adam challenged himself to flip this situation around. He used his assertiveness to stand up for his values of kindness, empathy, and openness. He walked confidently to the front of the plane and had a six-minute conversation with the lady who took away our phones and our dignity! (Okay, maybe I'm being a tiny bit dramatic). Anyway, after three minutes, she started crying, and two minutes later she was hugging Adam. I couldn't believe what I was seeing from the back of the plane.

Adam came back to our seats with both of our phones in his hand and related the openhearted conversation with the flight attendant:

"Ma'am, I don't know you, and you don't know us. But I wanted to come over here and tell you I'm sorry for what just happened. We are just trying to get to our destination after a very long and frustrating day. How my wife reacted was wrong, but I truly believe that if we could all first approach people with kindness, we could avoid situations like this in the first place and the world would be a better place. We are all human, and deep down we're all good people. I know you're kind and that you just want the best for all of us on this plane, and I assure you that my wife is also a beautiful person who didn't mean for any of this to happen. Can we start over? My name is Adam, by the way, and that's Michelle."

To which she responded, "I AM a good person!" And then she hugged Adam.

That day I learned two valuable lessons from Adam:

1. To fight with kindness

2. To trust your values as a way to stand up for yourself

But in order to put those into action, I need to practice assertiveness, which will build my confidence and give me the courage to express my thoughts in the most transparent and decisive way. Living with Adam has helped me recognize some of the traits and behaviors that we can all adopt to become more assertive people. Ready?

Assertive People Trust Their Judgment

This has nothing to do with pride, ego, stubbornness, or IQ. When assertive people know deep down in their hearts that something feels right for them, they fight for what they believe to be fair.

Let's say you find an insect crawling inside your food at a restaurant. That is a fact, it's wrong, and you obviously didn't put it there

(I hope). In that case, non-assertive people would just take the insect out themselves, request the check, and even ignore it ever happened. Why? They'd rather save themselves the uncomfortable conversation and continue with their lives. Who wins? Nobody. You didn't get a new meal or a discount, and the restaurant probably lost a customer. But when you decide to be assertive, you stand up for what's right and you put others to the test. Assertive people would speak up and say that there is something wrong with their food. On top of that, they would kindly suggest to be compensated for the restaurant's mistake. If the restaurant has a good culture and empowers its employees to make decisions, you, as a customer, won't only get a new meal and a discount, but also an extra something from the chef. Who wins? Everybody. You not only left the place feeling satisfied, but the restaurant won your heart and your loyalty, and you made sure that your server received a decent tip.

It's in the most challenging moments that we get to prove ourselves right or wrong, make it or break it. Take advantage of those moments to be the best version of yourself.

Assertive People Make Mistakes and Acknowledge Them

"I was wrong" is one of the hardest things we'll ever say, but at the same time it is also one of the most liberating statements. It is just a recognition that we are all human and that it is okay to make mistakes; in fact it just means that we tried. The best part? When we fail, and we publicly admit it, we make people trust us more.

For some reason, we are afraid to admit our flaws because we assume people will judge us negatively, and they will realize we are not who we say we are. But it is quite the opposite. When we let others know that we have failed, we show others our courage and our commitment to making good judgments about ourselves and others. This will earn other people's trust and respect.

Assertive People Don't Give Up Easily

When you know there is something to be done in order to fix a situation, and you are depending on someone else to do the job (a customer service representative, a professor, your boss, the IT guy)—and that person is not helping—what do you do? I usually say something like, "At least I tried!" and move on.

Assertive people know that if they try hard enough, they will get what they want, so they inform themselves (assertive people are pretty resourceful) and they try as many times and different ways as necessary.

I live with one of the most assertive people I know, and I have to admit that it gets embarrassing after the third or fourth try. Watching Adam be so persistent makes me cringe at times. But then seeing how he always gets what he wants, sometimes after the fifteenth attempt, makes me feel proud to be his wife, and I admire him even more. Trust me, I've seen him call an airline eleven times before we get our flight changed free of charge. *Who does that?*

Assertive People Value Their Needs

It's one thing to be a nice person, a caregiver, a mensch. And another one, very different one, is to be a people pleaser. Assertive people can be extremely nice and considerate without having to put their needs last. When we become people pleasers—because we either want to be liked, or we love to give too much—we are putting other people's needs first and our self-care last.

This may win you a few friends at first, but eventually, you will realize that this behavior will only lead to resentment, lack of self-respect, and low self-worth. The problem is that people around you will:

- Get used to being taken care of.
- Eventually take you for granted.
- Always assume that you are doing fine—so they will stop offering their help and support.

I see that this happens often with mothers and caregivers. Moms want to be there so much for their kids and their spouse that they forget to take care of themselves and ask for help.

Assertive people can identify when their needs are not being met, and they make sure to point it out as a way to let others know what they need. They don't simply assume that people around them are mind readers.

It is not easy to be vulnerable and say that we need more attention, love, appreciation, or help, but it is so necessary in order to make any relationship work.

Assertive People Don't Negotiate Their Values

In a situation where one needs to confront, debate, or demand, assertive people will not be afraid to stand up for what they believe in.

If you value authenticity as much as I do, you should not feel afraid when confronting a copycat. If you value honesty above all, you should confront a cheating partner with courage—clearly, that person is no longer what you need. And if you value kindness, you will make a point about it when you realize you are being treated poorly—and fear should be the last thing on your mind. While we're on the subject, go back to Chapter 4 for a moment: review your values, and remember a time when you had to stand up for yourself and didn't. Next time, trust and stick to your values and go for it.

An interesting exercise that can help you when arguing with someone you care about, is to think about the following questions before you even start the conversation:

- What specific results do I want to achieve by having this discussion?
- How do I want the other person to feel after the discussion?
- How do I want to feel after the discussion?

These simple questions can help us prepare better and have the right attitude and tone.

Assertive People Listen

There's a difference between hearing and listening. When you listen to other people you are actually paying attention, not only to what they say, but also to how they say it and what they mean. This is key when communicating with others. The best way to make the other person open up and consider our request is by making that person feel validated. When you truly listen, you get to address the conversation in a way that resonates with others, and by doing this they will be more willing to listen to you.

Empathy plays a big role here. Assertive people can put themselves in the shoes of the other person in order to speak their language and make the other person feel understood and respected.

Assertive People Don't Blame Others for How They Feel (Even When They Are Guilty)

Blaming and shaming can only bring out the worst in others. In order to address an issue and work on it, we should start by expressing how we feel, not how the other person is making us feel.

Instead of starting sentences with "You," start sentences with "I." And when negotiating, don't start by asking, start by offering. Also, don't say things like "you should." Say "I will" and hope that the other person will follow your lead.

Don't assume the worst in others from the get-go—that would be hopeless—assume the best and go from there. Because in the end, assertive people like to surround themselves with other assertive people, and I firmly believe that if we work hard enough on ourselves and develop our courage, we can all be one of those.

Assertive People Make Every Word Count

I usually start my emails with three HUGE paragraphs before Adam magically turns them into the seven most intentional lines you've ever read. And this goes beyond emails. If you see me about to explain something, sit back and relax; it will take me a few minutes to make my point. Whereas Adam can easily make a point very clearly in a matter of seconds. This is one of the traits I admire the most in assertive people.

To help you better communicate an idea next time around, I asked Adam to tell me the main things he takes into account when having an important conversation by email, phone, or even in person:

1. **WHAT IS THE OBJECTIVE?** Have your objective top of mind at all times so you don't deviate halfway through the conversation. This is what will allow you to be clear from the get-go.

2. **LEAVE OUT UNNECESSARY INFORMATION.** Stick to what matters most and leave out the small details at first.

3. **RESPECT THE OTHER PERSON'S TIME.** Be considerate of the other person's tight schedule when having a conversation or writing an email. The best way to do this is by going straight to the point and then wrapping up as soon as possible.

4. **DON'T DEMAND, REQUEST.** These are two very different ways of asking for something. When we demand we are not being respectful of the other person's situation, and we are asking them to adapt to our needs. ("Have this ready by tomorrow at noon.") That kind of language sounds condescending and will not be well received by anyone. When we request something we can be straightforward, yet considerate of the other person's needs ("If you could have this ready by noon tomorrow, it would be awesome!").

5. **GIVE SOLUTIONS, NOT PROBLEMS.** There will always be problems. There are those who will expect others to solve the problems ("Hey Jen, not sure what to do with this client. He's asking for..."), and there are assertive people. Assertive people would not email you or call you about a problem without first offering you a few good solutions ("Hey Jen, the client is asking for... What if we..."). This will make everyone's lives easier and more efficient.

6. **PREPARE IN ADVANCE.** Assertive people don't like to be caught off guard, so before meeting other people, they prepare themselves. They research the relevant person, topic, and industry in order to be well-informed and not waste time asking basic-knowledge questions. Also, they anticipate the other person's questions and potential responses when preparing for a meeting, which always makes them look good and well-prepared.

7. **BE INTENTIONAL.** This is the main thing that defines an assertive person. There is intentionality behind every word, every question, every observation, and every pause.

Courage

The most important thing when it comes to assertiveness is courage. Because when we go from being passive to being assertive, we may encounter some resistance—mostly from the people around us who are used to us acting a certain, expected way. At that moment, **the only person who can validate you is YOURSELF.** Only you can remind yourself of the reasons why you decided it was worth it to fight for what feels right for you. Only you can make others respect you. And only you can stand up for yourself. It will not be easy, but it will be 100 percent worth it.

Assertiveness is a muscle; we must practice it, even if it makes us uncomfortable. Because the more assertive we are, the closer we will be to getting the things we want, need, and deserve—and sometimes, even more. You've got this.

THE *only* PERSON
WHO CAN *validate* YOU
is YOURSELF.

FROM ONE HUNDRED NOS, TO "BUT, WHY NOT?"

Interview with Jia Jiang

Jia Jiang was terrified of facing rejection. He had decided to quit his job in marketing to become an entrepreneur, but his fear was keeping him from reaching out to investors to the point that he even considered quitting on his dreams.

One day, Jia decided to go on a journey where he committed himself to ask for one hundred of the wildest and most outrageous things and in the process become immune to rejection. What an awesome idea!

Some of my favorite examples are:

- Asking for a burger refill at a burger joint.
- Asking to be an Abercrombie model at the mall.
- Asking to borrow $100 from a stranger.
- Asking a police officer if he could drive his car.

And the one that went viral on YouTube:

- Asking the lady at the Krispy Kreme to re-create the Olympic logo with donuts. Which she did! And it looked AMAZING.

I learned about Jia when I was in the process of facing my fears, and I decided to reach out and hope he wouldn't *reject* me! He didn't. Jia was the sweetest, and we kept in touch over the years. I'm *so* glad he accepted my invitation to be a guest for this chapter! If someone embodies what an assertive person is, it's Jia! But it was not always this way.

MICHELLE: Has your level of assertiveness increased since you started challenging yourself?

JIA: For sure. I learned that if you really believe in an idea, it pays to be assertive. And it is not about forcing your opinion on others—it is about knowing how to explain yourself better so others can see your vision. It is about holding our ground and being okay with agreeing to disagree. I now stay cool and calm when debating an idea or explaining myself. I don't feel the need to dominate. On the contrary, [I establish] a framework with the right criteria to make good decisions when working with other people.

MICHELLE: How do you perceive rejection now versus before?

JIA: Before embarking on this rejection journey, I would constantly look for cues of acceptance. It was really hard to deal with having people disagree with me, so I constantly tried to avoid that situation. I'd do anything to avoid conflict! Rejection therapy made me realize that when someone rejects you, they are not rejecting YOU as a person, and that thought helps me deal with rejection much better today.

MICHELLE: Any advice on how to reject others?

JIA: When rejecting someone I give them alternatives instead of saying no. Then, I am actively helping other people and building relationships. I learned that saying no doesn't have to be the end of any relationship; it can even be the beginning.

MICHELLE: What do you do when you get rejected now?

JIA: I now know how to keep the conversation going instead of simply taking no for an answer. Think about it as a negotiation. I realized that rejecting something or someone is a natural reaction to human beings wanting to be in control. It doesn't mean the person hates me; it just means that I have to work through the initial negative reaction to get somewhere. Instead of running away I now ask why, and, "What can I do to make this happen?" That way I make the other person help me get where I want!

MICHELLE: What is your current mindset in regard to rejection?

JIA: I take rejection as a challenge, instead of something I must avoid. I actually want to get rejected! It's fun! Next time you ask for something, challenge yourself to get rejected instead of getting approval; it's not that easy sometimes!

MICHELLE: Can you give us one piece of advice for people who'd rather not try because they are terribly afraid of getting rejected?

JIA: When you decide not to try, you are not competing against rejection; you are simply rejecting yourself.

EIGHT Key TAKEAWAYS

Go to hellofearsbook.com to explore more activities that will make this chapter jump off the page.

→ Learn more about dialectical behavioral therapy (DBT) and rejection.

→ Watch 5 Gum's "Life Happens in 5" campaign.

→ Read Derek Sivers's book *Hell Yeah or No.*

→ Read the open letter I sent to American Airlines after the plane incident.

→ Watch Jia Jiang's TED Talk and read his book *Rejection Therapy.*

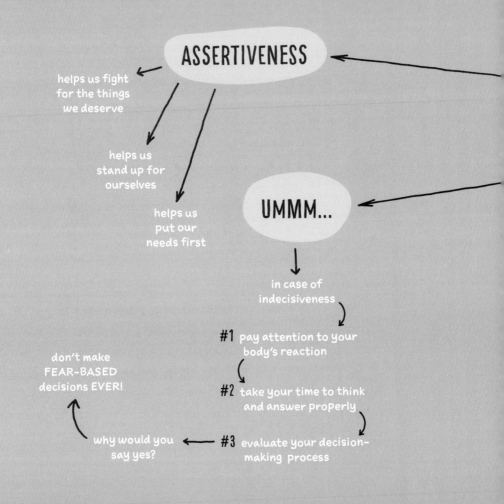

ASSERTIVENESS

helps us fight for the things we deserve

helps us stand up for ourselves

helps us put our needs first

UMMM...

in case of indecisiveness

#1 pay attention to your body's reaction

#2 take your time to think and answer properly

#3 evaluate your decision-making process

why would you say yes?

don't make FEAR-BASED decisions EVER!

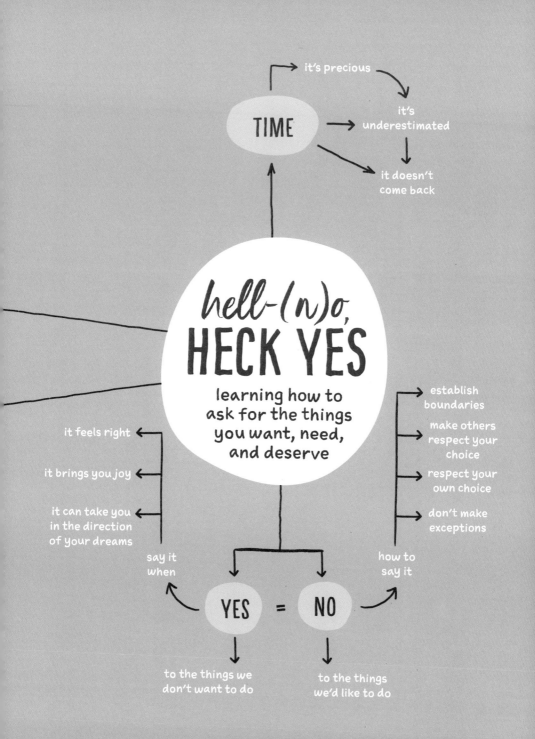

hello,
SUCCESS

HOW NOT TO SELF-SABOTAGE YOUR WAY TO SUCCESS

IF YOU MADE IT THIS far into the book, it's because:

1. You are really committed to making it in this world, and your only barrier has always been fear (but not anymore, baby!).

2. You are a finisher. You like to finish everything that you start. Good for you! You are *almost* there!

3. You just got the book and opened a random page and, well...here we are.

Truthfully, I've never finished reading a book. In fact, this book has to be the first one, in my entire life, that I finished. Yay! So, kudos to you for making it this far! There is only one fear left to discuss before you read the *last* chapter and make it big: **fear of success**.

"Wait, isn't that the same thing as fear of failure?" Glad you asked. And, no, it has *nothing* to do with the fear of failure.

Fear of success is something I experienced for the first time days after writing Chapter 8. I brought it up on social media, and turns out, it is a thing! After posting about the fear of success, my community started commenting and sharing their perspectives on this matter, and well...I was fascinated to the point that I decided to add another chapter to this book, all about this particular fear. Turns out, people are actually afraid to be successful for plenty of reasons, all very rational and relatable.

But first, can we please define success?

ACCORDING TO GOOGLE: The accomplishment of an aim or purpose. (Loveeee that the word *purpose* is in there).

ACCORDING TO MERRIAM-WEBSTER'S DICTIONARY: The attainment of wealth, position, honors, or the like.

ACCORDING TO SOCIETY: Being married, owning a home, having a stable job and at least two children, all before turning thirty.

ACCORDING TO SOCIETY (after the "influencer" boom started around 2015): Being married, owning a home, having a stable job and at least two children, all before turning thirty, and also having a side hustle, a ton of followers, and a juicer.

ACCORDING TO ME: Turning my passion into my full-time job and inspiring others to do the same.

Defining what success means for *us* is literally the most important thing we have to do in order to know where we want to go in life. It works just like Waze or Google Maps. In order to know which direction to go, you first need to put in the correct address.

The last thing we want is to be fooled by what society defines as success. In Chapter 7, I talked about focusing on *rewards* as our one tool to pursue our growth path. We can all agree money is a reward, right? No! It only becomes a reward if you value money. What are the things that YOU value? We need to ask ourselves this question to understand what we consider success.

So, please take a moment to write your own definition of success according to what you value:

Success is:

_____

_____

_____

_____

_____

_____

We will focus on the fears that hold us back from achieving ultimate career success and how to deal with the side effects that achieving your goals may bring.

SUCCESS = HAPPINESS?

Success is 100 percent personal. Your success can be HELL for others, and others' idea of success can be a nightmare for you. We have to stop defining success as something you can paint with broad strokes, like the *ideal* of having a ton of money, followers, fame, or a family that is #goals. Maybe, just maybe, you don't need all or even any of those things to be happy. For example, some people would absolutely hate to expose their life and have people following them around. Others would not want to *ever* get married. Some perceive having loads of money as a curse. But, for some reason, we have a really hard time accepting the fact that each one of us has a different definition of success, and we judge each other based on our own definition—or worse yet, society's definition of success.

Soon we start to compare ourselves with the people around us, to the point that we fool ourselves into wanting things that we actually don't. **Have you ever achieved something only to realize that it didn't give you the satisfaction you thought it would bring you?** You confused other people's idea of success with yours.

Success = happiness, but only when we reach OUR kind of success.

Two (Very) Different Views on Success

A few years ago, when I was invited to speak at an awesome event in Portland called World Domination Summit, I met Pete Adeney, or Mr. Money Mustache, as he calls himself. Hours before going on stage, I asked Pete what his topic was. His answer was unexpected:

"I shouldn't even be here, Michelle. My topic is about how I retired six years ago when I was thirty years old. My goal was to save enough money in my twenties to have a kid at thirty and spend the rest of my days playing with him and teaching him about life. And that's where I should be right now, with him, playing Frisbee or something, not here memorizing a bunch of slides!"

I thought his topic was so interesting! I couldn't wait to hear him speak. In fact, I thought he should totally do a TED Talk, but he insisted, "Hey, Fear Girl, you're not listening. My being here means doing the exact opposite of what I preach, so doing a TED Talk is the

LAST thing I want to do. In fact, I have rejected TED a few times already."

"But Pete, you can reach millions, and you could inspire them to change their lives with your epic story!" I said.

"I already do, Michelle. I have a blog with eight million readers a year! That is probably more than what TED can bring me, and it's something I enjoy doing from the comfort of my own home when my kid is asleep," he said.

The reality is that Pete and I have very different definitions of success. I wanted him to be successful my way, but what I didn't realize at that time is that he was already successful, in *his* way. He was right. If delivering presentations was something that didn't bring him joy because it meant being away from his son and the things he actually enjoyed doing, why would he want to be successful at that?

Since I asked you to define what success means for you a few pages ago, I now want you to define **what success is not**. For Pete, success was *not* about being an acclaimed speaker and traveling the world. And for me, success is *not* about retiring early in life.

So, write here the things that wouldn't signify success for YOU:

Success is not:

The *last* thing you want is to become successful at something you don't enjoy doing.

SKILLS VS. PASSION

Skills: the things we are naturally good at. The more we work on them, the better we get. **Passion:** the things that bring us fulfillment or joy when we practice them. We don't necessarily need to be good at them.

As kids, our parents are eager to uncover our skills. "He may turn into an amazing baseball player one day! He has a nice swing for a three-year old!" or "What if she becomes the next Taylor Swift? Listen to her sing!" As soon as a kid does something a tiny bit remarkable, some adults get all excited and insist on making the poor kid pursue whatever they seem to be talented in. But sadly, being talented at something doesn't mean we actually enjoy doing that thing.

So, as a future mom, my desire will be to help my kids identify their true passions and pursue them, instead of pushing them to become successful doing something they might be amazing at, but not happy with. In that case, they will be successful in my eyes, but not in theirs.

Now that we have defined what your success is (and isn't), let me tell you about the different fears that people associate with success, because they've affected my life tremendously.

NEW LIFESTYLE

Before moving to New York, before enrolling in the master's in brand-ing, before creating a viral project, before becoming an entrepreneur, and before living my success story. I was working in an office with a view of the ocean, from 9:00 a.m. to 7:00 p.m., Monday through Friday. I used to spend my nights working on freelance projects that I some-what enjoyed doing because they were branding-related, as opposed to advertising, and spent my weekends driving around Miami Beach with Adam in his Camaro. And he played baseball every Sunday with his brother and a team that he loved.

My passion projects were my videos. I used to take my GoPro to every event, trip, or celebration, and then I used to spend hours editing videos to share with my friends and family. I did one for our honeymoon, a few for my best friends' weddings, one when my first niece, Shira, was born, and another one when my first nephew, Josh, was born—#equality. Finally, I would edit yearly videos to celebrate our anniversary as a gift to give our future selves, year after year. Those were my personal favorites. I would combine all the experiences we had throughout the year in a fun fifteen-minute video that perfectly captured the essence of that year and the zeitgeist of the era as well.

And as you already know, we had our family nearby, and my friends as well.

That lifestyle is gone now.

When we decided to move to New York, pursue a different career, and accidentally make it in the Big Apple—WAY sooner than what we had anticipated—our life completely changed. And that is the ultimate fear related to success.

FEAR OF CHANGE

Some people like their life just the way that it is now. Yes, they do want to make more money, they wouldn't complain if they had some sort of recognition for their skills and their accomplishments, and they would be happier if more people wanted to use their product or read their content. But other than that, they like their life as it is! So, the thought of suddenly making it can be daunting because it would mean many changes:

- Not enough family or leisure time
- More exposure
- Greater responsibilities
- Change of lifestyle according to your new needs and possibilities
- Being perceived differently by your peers (and by yourself)

For me, that sounds exciting! But for some, it's quite the opposite. The truth is that **if you become successful at doing something that you weren't doing before, your life will change.** So, before embarking on a "this could actually work" kind of journey, consider if you would like your life if it ends up actually working!

WE HAVE to
BE OKAY
LEAVING *the* LIFE
WE ARE LIVING
to LIVE *the* LIFE
WE DREAM
of LIVING.

In my case, the only thing I truly miss from the lifestyle that I described earlier is having the extra time to work on those yearly videos I used to do for our anniversary. It's been a few years since I had the time to work on one of those, because working on that would mean not writing this book, not speaking over seventy times a year, not cultivating my community on Instagram, and not helping Adam build his brand. Time is limited, and for now I'm using my time to build my business from the ground up and live my life as happily as possible—understanding that we cannot have it all and being okay with that.

Do I miss living close to my friends and family? I do. In fact I visit them every two months. But do I miss having to work at an office, having a boss, and creating work that, for me, was meaningless? Heck no! There is nothing wrong with that kind of lifestyle—in fact, that could be a *dream* come true for some. But for me, it was the opposite.

We have to be okay leaving the life we are living to live the life we dream of living. Now read that again—and again—until you fully grasp what I mean.

I envisioned myself as a successful entrepreneur, a well-known speaker, and a thought leader. But in order to get there I had to sacrifice many things. Things I was okay giving up in order to attain other things. Things that gave my life more meaning and purpose. Things that fulfilled my definition of success.

These are some of the daily sacrifices I've made and the benefits they've brought me. Which of these would you be okay sacrificing?

WHAT I SACRIFICE	WHAT I GET
Weekends	Being my own boss
Living near family/friends	Living in NYC, our favorite place on Earth
Owning a car and a house	Total freedom to move around as we please
Babies	Fully focusing on our career for now
9–5 job stability	The opportunity to grow exponentially
Leisure time	Getting good stuff done
Routine	New experiences

EXERCISE

Imagine you set a pretty high goal for yourself for next year. One that has the potential to change your life. What would that goal be? Dare to dream big for this exercise. Maybe it's reaching one hundred thousand followers, launching a *successful* product or store, getting published, going on live TV, getting hired by the company of your dreams for the position of your dreams and the salary of your dreams, or being best friends with your idol. What is that goal?

My goal for next year is to:

Now, fast-forward and imagine that over the next twelve months you worked tirelessly to make it happen and...you made it happen! Not only did it happen, but it went better than expected! OMG YASSSS! Savor your success for a brief moment. Now double the size of your dream:

How do you feel?

 ANXIOUS EXCITED

Take a couple of minutes now to write down the positive and the not-so-positive ways in which your life will change now that you've achieved your goal:

POSITIVE CHANGE · NOT-SO-POSITIVE CHANGE

Do you still want to achieve your goal?

 HECK YES! UMMM, NOPE

If you answered "Heck yes!" keep reading! If the answer was "Ummm, nope," rethink your goal and do this exercise again until your answer becomes "Heck yes!" Or, read the story below to see how this exercise completely changed my perspective on what I thought success was for me.

In 2016, I had the opportunity to chat Sheryl, a true #GirlBoss who's the founder and CEO of a company that employs more than one hundred people in New York. She asked me a question:

"Michelle, how successful do you want to be? Do you want to make a good living speaking and traveling with your husband so you continue having the freedom you currently have once you guys start having kids, or, do you want to be high-level successful, meaning you start employing people and expanding until you have 50+ employees and this becomes your life? Because if this is the life that you want, you will have to sacrifice A LOT. Forget about putting your children to bed at night, forget about owning your time or life as you know it. Once you have people to manage, bills to pay, an office to maintain, life gets complicated. Don't even answer the question; just think about it."

Sheryl's question gave me **perspective**, and made us, Adam and I, value what we have now. It made us realize that we value our freedom and our time above all, and that maybe we don't need to become the next big thing to have an impact and still enjoy our lives. That's why it's so important that we define early on what we want out of life and what we don't.

But regardless of the level of success that we attain, not only will our lives change but the way we perceive ourselves will change as well, and that certainly can be scary.

NEW SENSE OF SELF

I'm not the same person I was five years ago before I decided to face my fears. I mean, I still have things in common with that person, but we are not the same. My personality remained the same, but my mentality changed significantly due to the experiences I've had, the things I've learned, the people I've been able to surround myself with, and the internal work I've done over the years.

Old Michelle was a dreamer.

NEW MICHELLE IS ALSO A DOER.

Old Michelle liked being rescued.

NEW MICHELLE LIKES TO BE CHALLENGED.

Old Michelle said "No thanks!" to new experiences and opportunities.

NEW MICHELLE SAYS "NO THANKS!" TO LIMITING BELIEFS.

Old Michelle sought approval to feel good about herself.

NEW MICHELLE SEEKS CONSTRUCTIVE CRITICISM TO WORK ON HERSELF.

Old Michelle cared about beauty.

NEW MICHELLE CARES ABOUT INFLUENCE...AND BEAUTY, SOMETIMES.

Old Michelle needed Adam for her to be all right.

NEW MICHELLE CARES ABOUT ADAM BEING ALL RIGHT.

Old Michelle liked pink.

NEW MICHELLE LIKES PINK (SOME THINGS STAYED THE SAME).

Not everything about this new Michelle is better. I also now have less patience than before, I'm less tolerant, more demanding, more careful with my time, and bossier for sure. But even with that, I like this new Michelle MUCH BETTER. And I'm 100 percent sure you will like your future successful self much more as well.

But will other people you care about like the successful new you?

Becoming this new person will have an impact on the people around you. Your close friends, family members, and especially your partner's life will change when your life changes. Maybe not drastically, but their relationship with you will change because you will not be the same.

This will not come easy. Truthfully, once you make it for the first time everybody around you who genuinely loves you will feel happy and excited for you. I mean, what would you think if suddenly you saw your best friend or your sister on TV being called an expert on something? You would feel proud probably! But what if, after that experience, three out of five times when you call this person either for advice or just to hang out, they tell you they are too busy running their new business, flying out to speak at a panel, or being interviewed for (or even running!) a cool podcast. How would you feel then?

Success will bring MANY new things into your life. Guilt being one of them, unless you learn how to manage it.

GUILT

Success can be pretty lonely, if you ride that wave solo. You will go from having a similar life to that of the people around you, to suddenly having the awesome life you envisioned. And the truth is that you will have opportunities that no one else in your circle will, and that can bring guilt to many, which can prevent you from enjoying the success you accomplished through hard work.

When my project hit the media, I was in the middle of doing my masters in branding and working full-time in advertising. The first day that I was all over the news, all of my friends, classmates, and coworkers shared the articles on Facebook—*"I know her!!!!"* was the caption.

The second day fewer people shared, and by the third day the only people sharing my news were my recent followers, people I had no idea existed. They say there is no one more loyal than an unknown follower; it's true. It's not that my friends don't love me or don't feel happy for me, but my success puts their goals and aspirations into perspective. "Will I make it someday? Do I even want that kind of success? Was it luck?" These are just some of the questions we ask ourselves when we see others succeed.

When this happened, when my friends stopped sharing my news or asking me about my new life, I experienced guilt, and that prevented me from enjoying my success.

- Guilt for achieving the lifestyle I always dreamed of
- Guilt for not being able to share it with my friends and family
- Guilt for being busy doing things that were only impacting *my* life
- Guilt for being happy

"When we lose our tolerance for vulnerability, joy becomes foreboding."
—BRENÉ BROWN, DURING *SUPER SOUL SUNDAY*

Brené Brown says that the only way to fight the terrifying emotion of joy is not by feeling guilt but by practicing **gratitude.** The people who experience joy are not the most successful, the most accomplished, or the most loved. They are the people who practice gratitude the most. I followed Brown's lead and started being grateful, not only for the good experiences, but also for the challenges in my journey and for the overlooked blessings I may have. I even challenged myself to find the good things in the crappiest days. That is when I needed to be grateful the most. And only then did I start to experience joy in my success.

Additionally, I decided to adopt an abundance mentality and share my success and the rewards of it with those around me. More success means more connections, more influence, more power, more opportunities, more credibility, more access, more resources—you get the idea. And all of those benefits can eventually help your friends and family as well. Now you can promote their products, recommend their services, connect them with the right people, invest in their businesses, and help them in countless ways, if you are up for sharing your success with those you believe in. Make them see that if you grow, they grow.

By this point my friends and family are already used to my new lifestyle, and they have never been prouder of me than they are today. Some people will disappoint you, but as I've heard: "Don't worry about people who aren't happy for you. They aren't happy for themselves either." Don't take it personally, and remember: It's okay to let go of people with whom your values no longer align.

People can highly influence our decision-making process—for good and for bad—but ultimately WE decide what to do and what not to do. Here's when it gets dangerous. We can be fully convinced to move forward with an idea, but right before we hit "send" or "upload," our fear starts to play games with our mind. We can be so afraid to succeed, for countless reasons, that we are even capable of sabotaging our own chances.

SELF-SABOTAGE

As I'm writing this section of the book, no kidding, Adam approached me to tell me that his online course is not ready to launch yet.

> **ME:** "What do you mean, not ready to launch? Videos are up, the website looks good, your strategy is set. What's missing?"

> **ADAM:** "I don't know, I think it can have more information, and I can do a better job explaining some of the concepts. I feel bad charging for this course as it is now. Maybe I give it away for free...and create a better course next time."

> **ME:** "Seriously? I'm writing about self-sabotage *right now*, and you are telling me this? Ten minutes ago, you were ready to launch! And suddenly, you started getting cold feet? Do you realize you are THIS CLOSE to sabotaging your own accomplishment?"

Our fears usually take over right when the launch date is approaching, and the most common question we ask ourselves is, "Is this good enough?" A question our superego loves to answer with a clear *nope*.

Our superego wants to keep us safe, remember? Its job is to avoid heartbreak, and it will do anything in its power to stop us from taking any risk that may lead to failure or rejection. When this happens, we embody one of these three personas, or all of them at the same time:

Persona #1: The Impostor

You convince yourself that you are no expert on this subject, so you must do some *more* research before you actually publish that blog post about this thing you are so passionate about.

Persona #2: The Undervalued

You convince yourself that your content or your product is only *somewhat* valuable, and you will feel better about yourself if you would just give it away for *free*.

Persona #3: The Perfectionist

You convince yourself that it is almost ready, but not there yet. So, you delay your launch date again and again, because there is *always* something you can review one more time and improve.

———

If you're thinking, "yup, that's me!" read these three truths that will encourage you to get over those limiting beliefs, and hit "upload!" or "send!" or "launch!"—on whatever it is:

Truth #1: You Know More Than Some People

You may not have a PhD from Harvard, but I can assure you that you know more about a certain topic than the people you are talking to. If that's the case, you tell me: can you share some value with them, or not? I'm sure you can.

For example, if you are working on an online course about finance (like Adam was), don't compare yourself to Warren Buffett! You'll definitely feel like a tiny ant in a giant's world. But, if you stop for a second to think about your audience—most of whom admire your knowledge in your chosen area—you should be able to understand that even though you are no Warren Buffett (or Lady Gaga or Steve Jobs or J. K. Rowling), you can still share tremendous value with others.

Truth #2: Your Idea/Product/Service Works for YOU

When we talk from experience, our arguments become waterproof. Everyone can argue that *their* way is the best, but no one can debate what has or hasn't worked for *you*. For example, instead of saying, "This is the *best* way to take care of your nails," just say, "This is MY way of taking care of my nails!" Inarguable!

This book is a pretty clear example of that. I have no background in psychology, human behavior, or fear, but I trust that my ideas are valuable because I experienced all of the things that I'm sharing in this book. Instead of spending months reading about fear from well-known psychologists or experts, I decided to pay close attention to my life and come up with insights from real experiences.

We have to trust more in ourselves and in our personal experiences, and express our ideas from that angle—"If it worked for *me*, it may work for *you*."

Truth #3: Everything Can Always Be a Little Bit Better

Nothing is ever finished. I bet that even Beethoven's symphonies can be improved! We can always edit things one more time and improve— THAT is the beauty of life! Accept this truth and give yourself a hard deadline to work on your projects and then launch. French philosopher Voltaire said, "Perfect is the enemy of good." Heck yeah it is! Sometimes our desire to be perfect prevents us from trying at all, and how far along are you getting when you second-guess every step? I would rather launch something good and improve as I go, than delay and delay the *perfect* product.

> "If you're not embarrassed by
> the first version of your product,
> you've launched too late."
> —REID HOFFMAN, COFOUNDER OF LINKEDIN

Those are the three truths I tell myself when I'm doubting my content or product. I'm not telling you these are the three absolutely mandatory things you have to do, I'm just saying these things work for me. You see what I did there?

If you are capable of moving past your worst thoughts by adopting this mindset, you will likely be closer to reaching success and fulfilling your dreams. Which is a fear in itself. And something I experienced on Day *101* of the 100 Days Without Fear project.

FULFILLING YOUR DREAM

Remember the big goal that I asked you to envision a few pages ago? Now imagine one more time that it materialized. You worked hard AF, and you made it happen! You celebrate, you savor your well-deserved success, and... *now what?*

There is nothing more terrifying to me than a fulfilled dream because it only means one thing: you now need to come up with a new dream. Turns out, life keeps going, and it is our job to continue reinventing ourselves. Otherwise, we could fall into the biggest trap of them all: the comfort zone. And remember the Abraham Maslow quote? "You will either step forward into growth, or step back into safety." When we achieve our goals, we can't just stay there, or we would be moving backwards!

The first time I experienced that was the day after I spoke at TEDx. I realized that my precious project was over and that I had no plan whatsoever. I went from having too much on my plate—a job in advertising, classes at the School of Visual Arts, facing daily fears, uploading daily videos and giving media interviews—to being in a limbo, trying to answer the question: "Now what?"

When my project hit the press around my fortieth fear, virality expert Karen X Cheng was kind enough to hop on a call with me to share a piece of knowledge that I will never forget: "Michelle, you are viral now. Enjoy it while it lasts, because in a few weeks no one will be mentioning your name on the news. My advice is to go to the root of what made your project so viral and successful, and turn *that* into a lifestyle and a business. What is it about your project that resonated with so many people? What is that universal truth that you uncovered throughout your 100-day project? Think about that."

In 2012, Karen went viral when she announced her resignation from Microsoft with a YouTube video of her performing a parody of "American Pie"—talk about authenticity! After that happened, she was SO intrigued by virality that she decoded the formula to get attention from the press and create viral videos. Shortly after, she started using that formula to create more viral videos for fun, and before she knew it, she was creating videos for renown brands such as Beats by Dre and Brawny. Karen turned her experience into a new business venture, but how could I do the same?

So, I kept asking myself, "Now what?" When in fact, the question I should've been asking was "Yes, and?"

"Yes, and?" embraces whatever just happened or whatever situation you are in, and it also asks for MORE. It's not about leaving your amazing accomplishments behind—it's about creating space for more growth and more success.

By asking myself the "Yes, and?" question, I was able to turn a personal project into a movement and a career, using *courage* as the base. Because the one universal truth I uncovered while facing my fears was that **courage is contagious.**

YES, I faced 100 fears, **AND** I'm now inspiring millions to do the same.

As scary as achieving a goal and having to reinvent ourselves again and again may sound, the reality is that after hitting a milestone we don't just go back to the drawing board and start all over again from zero. We build on top of our success with the new tools that we have, the new knowledge that we gained, and the new doors that have opened for us.

After being able to build on top of my successful project, I now trust that I am more than capable of reinventing myself as many times as needed.

TRUST YOUR FUTURE SELF

"So, Michelle, what are you going to do when fear is no longer ~trendy~? I mean, how many times can you give the same presentation?"

That question was not taking into account two things:

1. There are 7.53 billion people in the world. I highly doubt I can get to all of them in this lifetime.

2. The human capacity to innovate.

Sometimes when we create something and we show it to the world, we assume that everybody already saw it, and we feel bad putting it out there again and again. But the truth is that the people who already heard about it will move on, and there will always be new people who had NO idea you existed! Look, I was in the news for months, all over the planet, and still, every time I go to an event, 70 percent of the audience tells me that they had no idea who I was before. This means that once we achieve a goal, we don't need to move on *immediately* to our next venture.

The best way to fight the fear of fulfilling your dream (or shall I say, *my* best way to fight this fear) is by trusting in my future self. If I did something phenomenal once, I know I'm capable of creating phenomenal work again and again! I'm still the same creative person I was in 2015, but this time with way more opportunities, experience, and knowledge. So, PLEASE don't let other people's questions and fears get in the way of your success. Here I am, years later, still surprising audiences with my story at the same time that I'm reinventing myself daily with new ideas.

But ultimately, without *courage* there can never be *success*.

IT TAKES COURAGE TO BE SUCCESSFUL

The one thing the subjects of all of these chapters and the pursuit of our goals have in common is that they require courage.

We talked about:

- Living to the fullest
- Leadership
- Expectations
- Authenticity
- Criticism
- Failure
- Growth
- Assertiveness
- Success

Courage is the ONE thing that will take us from where we are now to where we want to be. And I can certainly inspire you, but only YOU can change your life.

Even though **my definition of success remains the same throughout the years, my goals evolve as I grow.** I discovered the importance of checking in with myself on a weekly basis and with Adam as a couple. I ask myself frequently if I am satisfied with my life as it is now. The moment the answer becomes no, I have the courage to switch gears and look deeper to reveal what my next growth move will be.

Two years ago, I would shed happy tears if you'd have told me where I'd be right now. I wouldn't have even believed you. To me, doing thirty paid talks a year was just a dream, and last year I did sixty (at twice the fee). This year it will probably climb to eighty. I feel we've accomplished SO much in so little time that it blows my mind. While we're currently enjoying traveling over one hundred times a year,

WE HAVE TO *trust*
THAT OUR *future* SELVES
WILL MAKE THE *best*
decisions FOR US WHEN
THE *moment* COMES
WHILE WE *continue*
DOING OUR *best*
IN THE *now*.

speaking to as many audiences as possible, we're also thinking about starting a family and being able to stay home more. Our goals have shifted from becoming the busiest speaker to coming up with ways to generate income without having to travel as much.

And that is okay! We are allowed to detour, to rethink our paths, to question our strategies and change our minds. **We have to trust that our future selves will make the best decisions for us when the moment comes while we continue doing our best in the now.**

Success = The Happiness of Being Yourself

NINE Key TAKEAWAYS

Go to hellofearsbook.com to explore more activities that will make this chapter jump off the page.

→ Read the post about the fear of success that gave me the idea to create this chapter (better yet, read the comments below the post!).

→ Watch Mr. Money Mustache's talk at World Domination Summit ASAP.

→ Watch some of my early videos (yes, including some of our anniversary videos).

→ Learn about "happiness anxiety" with Brené Brown and Oprah during their *Super Soul Sunday* conversation.

→ Read the article from Karen X. Cheng on the fascinating topic of virality.

→ Watch Elizabeth Gilbert's seven-minute TED Talk about what happens when you fulfill a dream.

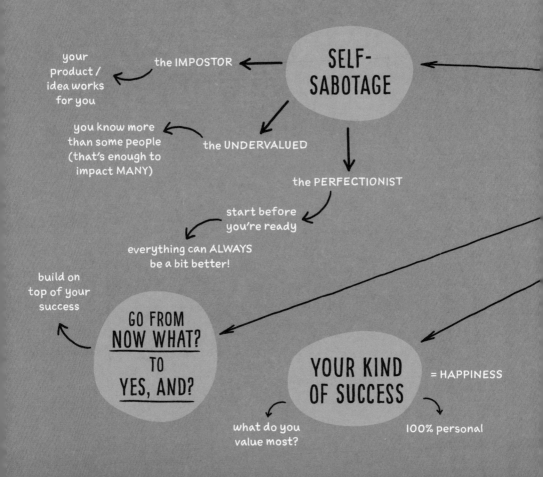

your product / idea works for you

the IMPOSTOR ← SELF-SABOTAGE

you know more than some people (that's enough to impact MANY)

the UNDERVALUED

the PERFECTIONIST

start before you're ready

everything can ALWAYS be a bit better!

build on top of your success

GO FROM NOW WHAT? TO YES, AND?

YOUR KIND OF SUCCESS = HAPPINESS

what do you value most?

100% personal

SKILLS VS. PASSION

things that bring us
FULFILLMENT (we don't
need to be good at them)

things we are
naturally good at

share the
rewards

help others
grow

GUILT

fight it with
gratitude

hello,
SUCCESS

how not to self-sabotage
your way to success

positive
changes

negative
changes

the ultimate fear
related to success

CHANGE

We have to be okay leaving the
life we are living to LIVE the
LIFE we DREAM of living.

hello, FUTURE

GROW THROUGH DIRT— REWRITE YOUR STORY

IN ORDER TO TALK ABOUT the future, first we have to understand the past.

My fears began way before I was born. It all started in the 1940s when my family was kicked out of their home in Romania and transported to concentration camps.

The Nazis took their home, their belongings, and their humanity. All because of one thing—their religion. Being Jewish at that time in Europe was a crime that resulted in severe punishment.

Long story short, my grandparents on my mom's side were sent to the labor camp in Transnistria in 1942. They were lucky because at that time there were labor camps and extermination camps—I'm sure I don't need to explain the difference. My grandparents were separated and sent to different locations. My grandma was able to stay with her son, who was two years old at the time. And my grandpa was taken under the wing of a Russian soldier, who took him home and kept him safe as long as he worked for him doing chores around the house. Thanks to him, my grandpa was able to bring food to my grandma and uncle every other week.

I grew up listening to these stories. My grandma didn't like to talk about this topic, but my mom would share the stories her late father shared with her. I never met my grandpa, but I know that thanks to him, they were all able to survive the camps. In 1947, the three of them hopped on a huge ship and traveled to Latin America along with thousands of other Jews who were also lucky enough, and strong enough, to survive the camps.

I learned about the Holocaust early in life, not only from my family but also from my Jewish school and my friends' families. Basically, everybody I knew had a story of survival, the kind of stories you would only see in movie theaters or books. Each one more incredible than next.

I grew up understanding that the world could be a very cruel place and that even though we may feel safe today, we may not be tomorrow.

In Venezuela, anti-Semitism was never a thing. Venezuela opened its doors to the Jewish people who came from Europe and made our families feel welcome immediately. But sadly, Venezuela was not the safest place for other reasons.

GROWING UP IN VENEZUELA

To be honest, I had a very happy childhood in Caracas, the capital. I had lots of friends, a big house, a beautiful community, and getaways to the beach every single weekend with my family. And even though Venezuela was not as dangerous as it became after 2010, the fear of getting robbed, kidnapped, or even killed kept me awake at night.

I remember from a young age being in my room not being able to fall asleep because I was afraid to let down my guard at night. Honestly, I never really feared monsters under my bed, ghosts, or the dark like other kids. It was real, dangerous people I was afraid of. I would stare at the hallway outside my room for *hours* just to make sure no thief would break into our house. No one ever did. And eventually, I started closing my door so I could fall asleep.

I lived pretty close to my school. It was no more than a ten-minute walk, but walking to school was never an option. I lived in a bubble pretty much. There was lots of security, lots of adults around, and lots of: "Pull up your window and lock your door, Michelle! This area is not safe!" Being cautious was enough to stay safe, but still scary for a fearful girl like me.

When I started driving at eighteen, I would get into my car, immediately lock the doors, and drive off. All of that in a matter of *seconds.* I didn't want to risk anyone getting into my car and kidnapping me.

As you can imagine, I lived in a constant state of anxiety throughout my childhood and adolescence, always making choices based on fear. Some studies say that the anxiety from being in the concentration camps can be transferred for generations, and I don't doubt it. It wasn't until I was in my mid-twenties and actively working on myself that I was able to change my mindset regarding fear, fulfill my ambition, and live fully.

If you are also allowing your past to hold you back and keep you from being the person you want to become, this chapter is for you. It will give you the tools and the mindset to **rebrand** yourself, **regain** your confidence, and **redefine** your future.

But first, let me tell you about the two individuals who shaped my personality.

MY PARENTS

My grandparents on my dad's side didn't endure the Holocaust. They left Europe as soon as things started to turn dark for the Jewish people in the late '30s. My dad was born in Panama, and the family immediately moved to Venezuela. He had a decent childhood without any kind of distress. In fact, he has always been a very confident person, showing me that there is nothing to fear and that life is an adventure that we must conquer. He's a heart surgeon for God's sake! In my world, that is BRAVE AF.

My mom grew up facing her parents' traumas and involuntarily adopted many of those herself, which shaped her personality. So besides being charismatic, empathetic, friendly, open, caring, and successful in her field, she is also an anxious person who is often afraid the worst is going to happen. And I don't blame her, because for her parents, it did.

From a young age I had the ambition, drive, and determination of my dad, but I also inherited some of the fearful behaviors of my mom. I started saying, "I'm afraid of..." often and stopped trying things that were outside of my comfort zone. She would sometimes push me to do things she knew I would enjoy, but you know what? Parenting is not easy because **kids don't do what you tell them to do. They do what you show them to do.** And I rarely saw her facing her fears, so why should I bother?*

BLAMING MY PAST

Being independent was never a goal of mine. I could spend *hours* with someone I didn't like as long as I didn't have to go somewhere by myself. Have you ever done that? Honestly, I loved having my parents do everything for me growing up and then my friends and Adam as a young adult. I used to think of myself as too fragile and unreliable. And I kind of liked being treated like a little girl and having people look after me. It made me feel protected at all times.

---

* If you were reading Chapter 1 and skipped forward to read this section, this is a good moment to stop reading this chapter and go back to Chapter 1! See ya!

It was all fine, until one day it wasn't.

After getting married, Adam and I considered having babies, but he wasn't too excited about it. He'd say, "Michelle, you say you want kids, but how are you going to look after them if you cannot even take care of yourself? What kinds of tools will you give your kids if you have no idea how to defend yourself? I don't want my kids to be as fearful as you are. How can you teach them courage? They will be just like you, and I love you, but I would like my children to be courageous." What he said hurt deeply, mostly because it was 100 percent true.

Ouch.

I had *no* argument against that. I started blaming my past: my grandparents' experience, and my mom's behavior. I found some sort of comfort in that. I defended myself by saying that it was not my fault that I was who I was. But to some degree, I enjoyed being that person. Who was I kidding?

In a recent conversation I had with my mom while I was visiting her, she took responsibility for my anxious personality for the first time. She said something so real and thought-provoking: "Michelle, I remember when you were little, I was always so scared that something bad might happened to you. I was always telling you 'not' to do certain things, 'not' to be too curious or too adventurous. I was always telling you to 'beware' and I treated you as if you couldn't take care of yourself. I'm sorry. Unintentionally, with my words and my actions I made you believe that you were not strong enough, capable enough, or trustworthy enough. My desire to look over you and protect you made you weak, scared, and gave you the idea that you always had to depend on others because you couldn't do things by yourself."

Whoa.

When kids are young, they need their parents to protect them. But most importantly to instill trust and confidence so when they grow up, they carry the tools their parents gave them on the inside and know how to look after themselves. When these tools are missing, we become dependent on others and feel extremely vulnerable, anxious, and in danger when left alone.

MISS INDEPENDENT

Two things that I learned by facing my fears: **I am way stronger than I thought I was** and **independence doesn't have to be scary.** In fact, it can be a blessing. It's a matter of, little by little, building our internal confidence by challenging ourselves to get outside of our daily comfort zone.

During my 100-day project I did all sorts of things by myself. I started by visiting a museum by myself. I went to a Broadway show by myself. I then went to a nice restaurant for dinner by myself, to the movie theatre, to a bar, and I even traveled to a new city by train for the whole weekend *all* by myself. It challenged me to nourish my independence and helped me connect with my inner thoughts, my desires, and the things I value the most. Also, little by little I started enjoying my own company. And you know what? Turns out, I'm pretty fun to be around! To the point that I started to celebrate my birthdays BY MYSELF! I realized that **personal growth can only come from**

within—and for that, we need to allocate some alone time at least a few times a week.

When I started facing all of my fears, I suddenly felt stronger, more confident, and trustworthy of myself. And that thought was scary. I started to feel as if I didn't need Adam anymore to function. I even wondered if our relationship could survive now that I didn't *need* him. These thoughts terrified me because I didn't want our relationship to change, but suddenly I was questioning the reason why I married him in the first place: was it because of fear or because of love?

Have you ever questioned that about some of the relationships you have? Think about your friends, your partner, your parents, your brothers and sisters—are those relationships based on love or need? How would your connection change if you didn't *need* a particular person anymore?

Little by little I realized that there was nothing to fear. I evolved, and so did our relationship. He was happy that I was being so independent, but above all, he was proud, and *admiration* is the one thing that makes him fall in love with me the MOST. Love, admiration, and similar values are everything you need to keep two people together— not furniture, not children, not a million photo albums, or a mortgage.

With time, I learned that I was not with Adam because I needed him, but because I truly wanted to be with him.

In fact, there have been times in our most recent story that I had to be the strong one, the one *he* could lean on and hold on to. That is what a true partner is. A partner is the person who will be there for you unconditionally when you need him/her and will have the courage to lean on you when he/she needs you. Because needing each other once in a while is okay, but it shouldn't be the foundation of any relationship.

That is why we need to teach our children to be independent—to walk by themselves, get up by themselves after they fall, speak up for themselves, earn a living, and make good choices by themselves. So, when they grow up, they don't depend on anyone, and they make choices based on love, not on fear or need. At least, that's how I'd like to raise my kids one day.

BREAKING MY FAMILY'S FEAR CHAIN FROM THE ROOT

When the 100-day project was finally over at the end of 2015, Telemundo contacted me to be a guest on one of their shows called *¡Que Noche!* (*What a Night!*). They wanted to highlight real people with inspiring stories, and at the end of the show they would give a surprise gift to every guest. I obviously accepted their invitation and was super excited to be on *live TV*.

That afternoon, as we drove to the Telemundo studios in Miami, Florida, I was wondering about the surprise they were going to give me. I was hoping that it was going to be one of those big checks people walk away with when they go on *The Ellen DeGeneres Show*, or a trip to Bali. I've always wanted to go there.

Adam, on the other hand, didn't seem too excited, and he was even trying to bring down my expectations as if he knew what the surprise was all about. Since I'm such a bad actress, and I easily show my feelings and thoughts without realizing it, he BEGGED me to act in case I didn't like my surprise. I started watching videos on YouTube to see how people react when they receive something exciting. There was a lot of face touching and sentences like, "I can't believe it" or, "I'm SO honored" or even, "I have literally no words!"

Minutes before going live, the producer of the show walked with me to the main studio where the presenters were interviewing the person that was going before me. It was freezing there, and I was SOOO nervous to be on live TV and embarrass myself somehow. And **my fear came true**.

The interview went horribly wrong. I suddenly forgot how to speak Spanish (my first language) and started using many words in English, which I shouldn't have. I was just so nervous that I couldn't think well. And then the time of the surprise came:

HOST: Michelle, your grandparents are from Poland, right?

ME: Yeah...

HOST: Well... As a surprise, we want to give you a trip to... POLAND!

Poland?

All I can remember is looking back and seeing the word *Poland* flashing across the gigantic screen behind us, with the Polish flag illustrated inside the letters and a photo in black and white from an old town in Poland in the background. So, I did what I learned that afternoon: I started touching my face and saying things like, "Wow, I can't believe it, I have no words. I guess I'm going to Poland."*

I was so thrown off and they could totally tell, but they didn't explain to me why the heck they were sending me to Poland. They didn't say that they wanted me to join the International March of The Living, a powerful event that occurs once a year where thousands of people march together from Auschwitz to Birkenau, two of the deadliest concentration camps in Europe.

Adam had to explain that to me once the show was over. Turns out that HE had been planning that surprise with them for the longest time.

ALIVE

I knew that visiting the concentration camps in Poland was a thing people did. I just never considered doing it myself. I thought I was not going to be strong enough to handle that experience. But in May 2016, we flew to Poland and days later we joined the International March of The Living. And that day I felt...*alive.*

Being inside of one of the most destructive camps, where millions

---

* No exclamation points needed because I didn't use any when I responded to their surprise. I'm such a bad performer.

of innocent Jews from all over Europe died, gave me perspective. And it was not the kind of perspective I was expecting.

I thought that being there was going to make me feel more resentful, powerless, and disgusted by humanity than I've ever been. But it was the opposite. Being there showed me that there is always hope, and that the good will prevail. I felt proud to be Jewish that day because us being there meant that WE won, and they didn't—we were stronger, united, and unbreakable. Today we are still here, making history. That made me feel optimistic, happy, and at peace. And optimism is the antidote to fear.

Traveling to Poland and visiting the concentration camps is something every human should do, at least once in their life. I know that one day I will take my children with me, and I hope that they take theirs. History is not meant to be forgotten; history is there to teach us, but it is up to us to learn and then teach those lessons to others so we don't repeat our ancestors' mistakes.

You're either history, or you're making history.

What is your story? What do you carry as baggage? And, is it yours or is it someone else's? My baggage was full of my fears—my mom's fears and my grandparents' fears. The goal is not to make the baggage disappear—or pretend it was never there in the first place. The only way to actually break free from our past is by acknowledging it and facing it headfirst—just like I did by visiting the camps. As I was there, I tried to feel every single emotion to the fullest, the good ones and the bad ones.

While my grandparents escaped the camps and never looked back,

I voluntarily visited them. While they kept quiet, I spoke openly about it. And while they lived in fear thinking that the worst was always going to happen, I decided to fight my fears with positivity. So, don't try to escape from your experience. Instead, immerse yourself in it. And then, transform it as a way to redefine your present and your future. Keep reading to learn the eight steps that will allow you to do this.

MY STORY GAVE ME PURPOSE

I'm so thankful to Telemundo for giving me the opportunity, and the push I needed, to go full circle and tackle my fears from the root. Being there gave my life even more purpose.

I thought of my grandparents, who intentionally decided to survive—not that everybody had that choice. **My grandparents could've died if they wanted to**; it was easier to die than it was to live inside the camps. But they chose to fight. They chose to live.

For the first time in my life I thought of my grandparents as strong and brave and even realized that I have some of that blood in me. I too can become a strong and brave person myself. I realized that **my grandparents fought hard for me to be here today**.

That thought made me feel important, as if I have to make my life count. I mean, they didn't survive the war for me to waste my life doing meaningless things. They survived for a reason, and I want to make it worth their while. At that moment, I decided to dedicate my life to empowering others and, most importantly, to empower myself and lead by example. Just like they made the choice to live, **I'm making the choice to make an impact on others and make this life count.**

So, I ask you: How are you going to make your life count? How are you going to commemorate that you are alive?

You matter, your life matters, and the dent you decide to make in this world matters tremendously. My wish for you is to live your life with purpose.

GROW THROUGH DIRT

You know, I could be pissed about my story, about what my grandparents had to go through, and about what my mom went through living with her parents. But thinking about it, THAT struggle is what brought me to where I am today. THEM going through all that $#!t gives ME the motivation to kick ass today and be my best self.

So, what if you could OWN your story, flip it around, and make something out of it?

"Echame tierra y veras como florezco."
("Throw dirt at me and watch me bloom.")
—FRIDA KAHLO

The dirt is the discomfort we have to go through in order to bloom.

The dirt could be a parent who didn't give you the tools you needed growing up. It could be an unfortunate childhood, the financial situation in your household, the war, drug issues, health issues, mental illness, the dangerous country you were raised in—you name it.

From Cancer to Greeting Cards

When illustrator and copywriter Emily McDowell was in her early twenties, she went through an experience that shook her. Instead of figuring out life, work, and adulthood like other twenty-four-year-olds, she was diagnosed with Stage III Hodgkin lymphoma. For the next eight months of her life, chemo and radiation kept Emily busy.

During her talk at World Domination Summit, Emily shares that what hurt her the most when she got diagnosed with cancer was not cancer itself and the discomfort of undergoing chemo. It was the fact that the people she cared about the most were the ones who distanced themselves from her the most. She felt lonely and unworthy of love.

Ten years later, Emily had another encounter with cancer when a good friend of hers got diagnosed. That is when she clearly understood that the *real* reason why people fade away from those who are sick is not that they don't want to be there. They do, more than anything, but they just don't know how to deal with or what to say to a sick person. **Fear prevents us from doing what we actually want to do: help.**

"Being sick is alienating," Emily says, "because you are still the same person you were before you were diagnosed, but no one you know can relate to you in the same way as before." And comments like "everything happens for a reason," sadly, are not helpful.

Recognizing this truth about humanity is what drove this creative copywriter to illustrate a series of what she calls "empathy cards" for "the relationships that we actually have." Some of the cards read:

"Please let me be the first person to PUNCH the next person who tells you that everything happens for a reason. I'm sorry you're going through this."

"You're not a burden. You're a HUMAN."

"There is no good card for this. I'm so sorry."

"If this is God's plan, God is a terrible planner. (No offense if you're reading this, God. You did a great job with that other stuff, like waterfalls and pandas.)"

And I can keep going, on and on.

Emily was able to transform her experience and grow a successful business from there. Through her cards she is now helping people all over the world support their loved ones when they need it the most.

The truth is that we ALL can bloom, but **blooming is entirely up to us**. Only WE can water ourselves.

Water: Eight Steps That Helped Me Bloom

There are many ways to water ourselves as a way to make something out of the dirt. These are the steps that helped me, and will hopefully help you.

1. Envision Your Change

We need to believe it is possible to grow from dirt, instead of living our entire life stuck in it. Do you see it? For a few moments try to envision the person you'd like to become mentally, emotionally, and physically. Every reality starts with a vision. I knew I wanted to become a braver person, an example for others, and a thought leader, but I was none of those things just a few years ago.

I want to become:

_____

_____

_____

_____

_____

2. Help Yourself

Once you convince yourself of that possibility, you must seek help, which is the healthiest thing we can do. You can start by reading self-help books, watching TED Talks online about other inspiring stories, going to therapy (which, as you know, has helped me A LOT), having an accountability partner, or even finding a support group related to your needs. Detox your social media feed ASAP, unfollow the toxic people or influencers who make you feel like your life is crap, and start following more real people with real advice. This way, you will not only envision your success story, but you will also feel empowered to pursue it. If others have done it, why can't you?

3. Define Your Path

How can you use your experience to make an impact? In my case, I wanted to become a speaker and share my message so more people could change their perception of fear. One of my goals was to speak to the younger generation and tell them all the things I wish someone would've told me when I was their age in the same way that Emily created the product she wishes would've existed when she was going through cancer. Maybe you want to teach something no one taught you or become the boss you never had or create a documentary you wish existed or a book that would've helped *you* years ago. **If you could do something for your younger self, what would you do?**

4. Get to Work

This step is to work on YOU. Once you define what the *new you* wants to do or be, you must develop the skills you need before you start putting them into action. Watch online courses, enroll in school, surround yourself with experts in the field, interview people—anything you can do to become a better version of yourself and uplift your confidence. For example, when I decided to become a speaker I enrolled in Toastmasters International—an organization with chapters all over the world for people to practice their public-speaking skills and learn from each other. I also read a book called *The Wealthy Speaker 2.0* with practical steps and tools. And I watched hundreds of TEDx Talks, not just to get inspired, but to learn from other great speakers. I also attended an event in California called Rock the Stage; its founder, Josh Shipp, now manages all of my youth-related events. These things gave me the confidence to start charging for delivering my message on stage for companies, organizations, and schools all over the world. Yes, I do it for a purpose, but I'm now also clear about the value that I bring to the table.

5. Shift the Focus

Are you excited—or terrified—to put all of those ideas into action? Newsflash: either way, it's not about you at this point. So, whether you feel excited or terrified, remember that whatever you are doing is for the benefit of others, which is a thought that helps me SO MUCH. Whenever I'm about to speak in front of a crowd, I think to myself: *Remember, it's not about you , it's about your message and the people who are here to listen.*

If you decide to become a chef, think about the experience you can give your customers. Or if your calling is to become a photographer, think about the memories you'd capture for your clients. Whatever we decide to do can have a long-lasting impact on others, so this is the moment where you stop focusing on yourself and focus on whoever is listening, watching, reading, or buying. Believe it or not, **you have the power to change someone else's life**—we all do—so use that as your motivation, leave your fear behind, and go for it. *What's the best that can happen?*

6. Always Remember

It doesn't matter how successful you get at doing this, never forget *why* you started and *where* you started. This will keep you grounded and focused, and it's the only thing that will give you the *purpose* to continue doing this EVERY. SINGLE. DAY.

7. Be Forgiving

We can accept or reject reality; either way the facts will not change. But the moment we decide to **accept** and **forgive** our past, we will be able to move past it, pun intended. Maybe it's someone else you have to forgive, or maybe it's yourself. Whoever held you back and gave you dirt needs to be forgiven. Forgiving is letting go. It's flipping the page. It's moving on. Forgiveness can happen externally or internally. Maybe that person is no longer with us; in that case, find forgiveness in your heart. And if they are still around and you want to literally forgive them, don't hold back. Remember, this is for you, and it's necessary. Holding grudges keeps us attached to people and situations; this is the time to break free.

8. Change Your Future

When we envision our future, we work on ourselves, we generate impact, and we let go of our past by owning our story: we become **unstoppable**. Each one of us has the possibility to change our own life and create our own luck. It's a matter of taking charge of our future selves now. Remember, we can become the hero of our own story, or the victim—it's up to us.

FUTURE

Honestly, I can't say that I was able to break my family's fear chain. Not yet. That will be the result of all the hard work I'm doing right *now*. Only my kids, in the future, will know if I did a good job raising them. I don't want to be the perfect mom, because that would give them unrealistic expectations. I want to be as human as possible so they can relate to me and be proud of my journey. I won't pretend to be fearless as a way to keep my fears from them. My goal is to show my kids that I do have fears, but also, that I'm willing to work on myself and face my fears head-on.

The important thing is to never let our fears get in the way of our passion, our ambition, and our goals. My guess is that if I give my kids that example, we'll do fine.

FINAL EXERCISE

I encourage you to write here a short letter to your future self. Write the current date and the date you want to open this letter in the future. **Make a commitment to yourself.** Let your future self know that you will work hard now to make her or him proud later. And then, fold the page in half and use a sticker to close it. Also, put a reminder on your phone for the day you wish to open this letter, so you won't forget. This could be a one-year commitment, a three-year commitment, or even a ten-year commitment—you choose!

Putting things in writing has enormous power. It gives us clarity on our goals and the confidence that we can make them happen. It also helps put our ideas into the universe and serves as a promise that we make to ourselves. What can be more sacred than that?

OPTIONAL: Attach a picture of your current self to this section and use this as a time capsule.

Now go out there and put everything you learned into action so you too can pursue your passion, make choices that work for YOU, become your most authentic self, and go confidently after your dream, so when that moment comes for you to open this chapter again, you'll say, "Michelle, you were so right." Because you know what? **You deserve to live your best life.**

Sometimes the things we want the most are just one act of courage away.

Dear future self,

LETTER WRITTEN ON: /   /

DO NOT OPEN BEFORE: /   /

Sometimes
THE THINGS WE
WANT THE MOST ARE
JUST ONE ACT OF
COURAGE AWAY.

TEN · Key TAKEAWAYS

Go to hellofearsbook.com to explore more activities that will make this chapter jump off the page.

- → Watch my disastrous interview on Telemundo's *¡Que Noche!*
- → Watch the video of our experience at the International March of the Living.
- → Read some of my favorite self-help books (list on hellofears.com).
- → Enjoy a video of me spending my birthday by myself.

- → Learn from others who were able to grow from dirt.
- → Take a look at all of Emily's empathy cards and buy her book *There Is No Good Card for This.*
- → Send your future self a letter.

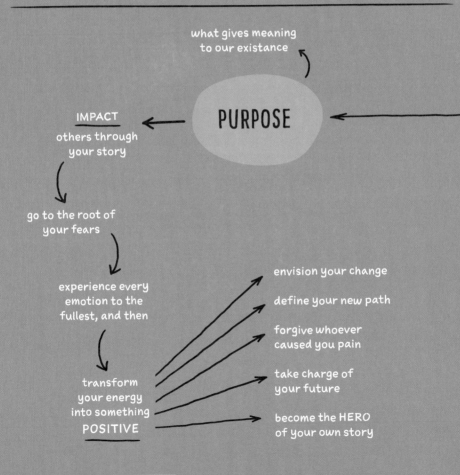

what gives meaning
to our existance

IMPACT
others through
your story

PURPOSE

go to the root of
your fears

experience every
emotion to the
fullest, and then

transform
your energy
into something
POSITIVE

envision your change

define your new path

forgive whoever
caused you pain

take charge of
your future

become the HERO
of your own story

builds SELF-CONFIDENCE

gives us FREEDOM

creates relationships based
on LOVE instead of NEED

can only come
from within

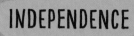
INDEPENDENCE

PERSONAL
GROWTH

hello,
FUTURE
grow through dirt—
rewrite your story

"Every flower has to
grow through dirt."
—FRIDA KAHLO

blooming is
entirely up to us

only we can water
ourselves

"Michelle Poler's real accomplishment has been—and continues to be—her growing awareness of her own remarkable power and determination and strength, and her extraordinary generosity in selflessly imparting what she has learned to others."

—DEBBIE MILLMAN ON *HELLO, FEARS*

AFTERWORD
by Debbie Millman

WHEN I FIRST MET MICHELLE Poler in 2014, it seemed as if she was afraid of everything. She was afraid of the subway. She was afraid of spiders. She was even afraid of frying food. In fact, she was afraid of frying *and* flying. She was genuinely afraid of so many things, I wondered how she had managed to muster up enough courage to move to New York to attend the graduate program I chair in branding at the School of Visual Arts. Frankly, it seemed unfathomable.

I didn't find out about Michelle's myriad fears until well into her academic journey, during a course I teach titled "A Brand Called You." While my program at SVA is primarily dedicated to understanding the many components that make up corporate and consumer branding, "A Brand Called You" is fundamentally about how students choose to position themselves in a competitive marketplace when they graduate, and how their understanding of themselves can help or hinder their own success. The centerpiece of the class is the completion of an exercise titled #The100DayProject. Originally created by Michael Bierut at Yale University, students are required to undertake a creative endeavor that is related to what they have learned about their own, self-imposed limitations or beliefs and are capable of repeating every day.

It didn't surprise me that Michelle wanted to do something related to her many fears. What did surprise me, however, was the ambition she revealed in her effort. She had plans to create YouTube videos! She envisioned jumping out of a plane! She wanted to dance in Times Square! I cautioned her not to push herself *too* hard; I didn't want her to burn out before the 100 days had passed.

I needn't have worried.

I've been lucky: I have had many exceptional students in my two-decade tenure as a teacher. I've had students that are now extremely successful brand consultants, brand managers, art directors and designers; I have had students that have started their own lucrative brands; I have had students who have become leaders of global firms, and I have had students who have become excellent teachers and mentors to others.

But I've never had a student like Michelle.

Let me be clear: Michelle's 100-day project was really no different than the hundreds of other projects that my graduate students have undertaken over the years. Yes, she made some excellent, entertaining videos and she was exceptionally media savvy. Yes, she went wildly viral. But we've had many other student projects go viral over the years at SVA. And there is no doubt we will continue to have many projects go viral in the future.

What makes Michelle's trajectory so singularly outstanding is what she has done *since* she completed her 100-day project confronting her many, many fears.

Not content with resting on the laurels of her viral success, Michelle has continued her work. She's examined and reexamined not only her fears, but her foibles and her flaws and her failings. And in the five years since she has graduated, she has not stopped striving to understand the resilience of the human spirit.

Michelle Poler's real accomplishment has been—and continues to be—her growing awareness of her own remarkable power and determination and strength, and her extraordinary generosity in selflessly imparting what she has learned to others.

—Debbie Millman

OCTOBER 2019

what's the **BEST** *the* **THAT CAN HAPPEN,** *if the* **WORST** **HAPPENS?**

ACKNOWLEDGMENTS

JUST AS I WAS ABOUT to finish writing this book, I had a session with my therapist. She has been helping me along the way by reviewing my chapters and giving me her valuable feedback. So, naturally, during our session we were discussing my expectations regarding this book. In that moment I admitted to her that I had pretty high expectations and that I was *terribly* afraid of this book being a flop.

Suddenly, she asked me to do something that I never saw coming: write a letter to myself answering the following question: "What's the BEST that can happen, if the WORST happens?"

Whoa.

I immediately opened my eyes really big and said, "No way." The discovery stage and the denial stage both hit hard in a matter of seconds. My fear in that moment was by even considering it a possibility,

I would be attracting the worst. I'm all about visualizing only the positive as a way to attract it, so that exercise threw me off completely. But she challenged me to do it, and I do love a challenge.

Anyway, I decided to give it a go, and I'm going to share the letter with you because it helped me tremendously in ways that I never could have anticipated.

DEAR MICHELLE,

Congrats! You wrote your first book, and it's out there. That is already a HUGE accomplishment. I mean, not everybody gets an offer from a publisher, AND an advance—on their FIRST book! Thank you, Erin Niumata and Josh Shipp for making this happen. Plus, Sourcebooks? The largest WOMAN-owned independent publisher in the world! What else can you ask for?

The best part: You enjoyed the process like NO OTHER! For NINE months you woke up FULL of purpose and overly excited to keep writing your book. Remember how everything else in your life was a distraction and an inconvenience? You just found so much *joy* in writing that you were not even excited the day you finished your book.

Don't forget how PROUD you were of yourself with every page and every chapter. You were continually surprising yourself. And *that* is more important than anyone's opinion.

You not only enjoyed writing the book. You also enjoyed the system you built around it. You cared so much about giving this book depth and professionalism that you reviewed every chapter with your hubby Adam Stramwasser, your therapist Daniela Sichel, your friend Stephanie Essenfeld—also a therapist—and your cousin Kevin Montello, who helped with the humor and the grammar. And not to mention Grace Menary-Winefield, your editor, who supported you AND challenged you on every chapter. You couldn't ask for a better human to work with—and I bet you miss the back-and-forth you had with her every day. How lucky you are that you got to work with such a remarkable team at Sourcebooks, from Meg Gibbons, who made sure this book was everything you ever dreamed of, to the incredible design team who had your back: Jillian Rahn, Brittany Vibbert, and Kelly Lawler. Lastly, Cassie Gutman, as the production editor who helped Meg and Grace! So much #womenPOWER! ☀

Finally, you should be exceptionally thankful for your @HelloFears community, all those readers who volunteered their time to give their honest feedback, and the designers who pitched their beautiful cover ideas for you to have options.

Don't forget about how during the process you became so much closer to your mom, Beatriz Poler-Bernstein. Remember all the great ideas she gave you for the chapter about failure and the one about rewriting your story. It was when you visited her in Panama that she opened her heart to admit her role in your fearful upbringing. And with tears she told you how incredibly proud she is now. It was a vulnerable and powerful moment you will never forget.

Also, don't forget how in love Adam was with you during the whole process. Remember the countless times he told you how proud he was as he watched you write nonstop for months? He deeply admired your commitment, your resilience, and your drive. He kept saying: I would NEVER be able to write a book! But you know he would.

All of this not only made writing this book so worth it, but it also made it an unforgettable experience.

Even if it totally flops, and only a few people buy it, or if it doesn't make it to Amazon's Top 100 list, or if it didn't help grow your online community, or even if you couldn't get the people you admire the most, like Brené Brown, Rachel Hollis, or Oprah, to share it, that's okay. They didn't get to where they are with their first books either.

Plus! You're only thirty-one years old, girl! You have an entire life ahead of you where you'll get to use what you've learned and put it in practice.

You are UNSTOPPABLE.

I have the utmost confidence that this is just the beginning of a very promising future for you. So keep hustling with that same passion, and above all, make sure you always enjoy the ride!

LOVE,
Michelle

SPECIAL THANKS

The people listed below donated their time and their skills to improve this book, and some even pitched beautiful concepts for the cover. I am incredibly grateful and honored for the Hello Fears* tribe. This book is for YOU:

Karla Aguirre	*Jenifer Blanco*	*Kenia Chávez*
Sofia Altuna	*Crisel Borges*	*Angela Crosby*
Andreina Atencio	*Vanessa Buelvas*	*Gaby La Cruz*
Eliana Barousse	*Elandra Burton*	*Jessica Czamanski*
John Beede	*Vanessa Cabello*	*Joelle Daccarett*
Adriana Beracha	*Tittina Del Carmen*	*Natascha Fernandez*
Flor Benassi	*Laura Castellano*	*Laura Doffiny*

---

* Special thanks to Nir Eyal for giving me the excellent idea to include my precious community here. I'm hooked, man!

Michelle Faraco

Cindy Foo

Fernanda Fuschino

Ailyn Esayag

Linnea Fritjofsson

Aileen Gartner

Ana Guerra

Cecilia Hahn

Cristina Hamana-Maza

Emma Heinrich

María Heredia

Karerina (Kare)
   Hernandez

Tere Hinojosa

Linsey Hugo

Matilyn Jones

Laura Jorge

Mauren Kaufmann

Ana Lara

Adriana Lindenfeld

Carolina Maggi

Orly Margulis

Elizabeth Martinex

Iwa Martinez

Amaranta Martinez

Yessica Márquez

Evelyn Mezquita

Dariana Moreira

Franz Moricete

Juanil Muñoz

Emily Norgaard

Mariana Olivares

Adriana Ovalle

Fabiana Parra

Andrea Parra

Lianett Perez

Erika Del Pozo

Marisa Quiroz

Martha Riessland

Ana Rincon

Vanesa Romero

Daniella Rondon

Nathalie Rodrigues

Jessica Rodriguez

Paola Rosales

Adriana Russián

Rocío Salinas

Roxanna Sarmiento

Alejandra Schatzky

Lesly Simon

Elizabeth Slimak

Ly Smith

Carolina Stone

Melva Suarez

Jennifer Taurel

Lisbeth Tolentino

Andrea Tredinick

Sue Varma, MD

Vianny Velásquez

Gary Ware

Margaret Zorrilla

Ashley Chui

Antonia Figueiredo

photo by ASHLEY CHUI
Illustration by ANTONIA FIGUEIREDO/AF.ILLUSTRATIONS

ABOUT THE AUTHOR

BORN AND RAISED IN CARACAS, Venezuela, Michelle Poler is a creative and passionate fear facer, keynote speaker, social entrepreneur, and branding strategist.

Michelle was accustomed to living with fear, but when she moved to New York to pursue a master's degree in branding at the School of Visual Arts, she quickly realized that the Big Apple was not for the fearful. In order to change her approach to life, Michelle decided to face 100 of her fears in a period of 100 days, uploading every experience to YouTube, where the project quickly became a viral phenomenon.

Facing her fears took Michelle to a TEDx stage, and this decision marked the beginning of her speaking career. Since then, she has given talks at companies such as Google, Facebook, LinkedIn, Netflix, Microsoft, P&G, Toyota, Coca-Cola, Yum! Brands, Wells Fargo, and many more, as well as inspired more than 100,000 students from all over the world at schools and leadership organizations.

Michelle and her husband, Adam, travel about 120 times per year, and as they do, they record a Spanish-language podcast, *Desde El Avión* (*From the Plane*), as they fly from event to event.

Besides creating content for the podcast, Michelle manages her Hello Fears community on Instagram (@hellofears), empowering thousands to step outside their comfort zones and tap into their full potential every day.